# LOGIC GAMES for Clever Kids

Puzzles and solutions
by Dr Gareth Moore
B.Sc (Hons) M.Phil Ph.D

Illustrations and cover
artwork by Chris Dickason

☆

Designed and edited by Tall Tree Ltd

☆

Cover design by Angie Allison

# LOGIC GAMES for Clever Kids

Buster Books

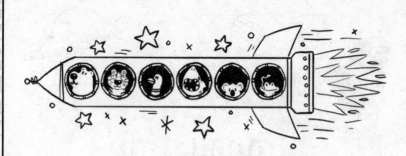

First published in Great Britain in 2020 by Buster Books,
an imprint of Michael O'Mara Books Limited,
9 Lion Yard, Tremadoc Road, London SW4 7NQ

W www.mombooks/busterbooks
f Buster Books
🐦 @BusterBooks

Puzzles and solutions © Gareth Moore

Illustrations and layouts © Buster Books 2020

A CIP catalogue record for this book is available from the British Library.

ISBN: 978-1-78055-662-8

2 4 6 8 10 9 7 5 3 1

Papers used by Buster Books are natural, recyclable products
made from wood grown in sustainable forests. The manufacturing processes
conform to the environmental regulations of the country of origin.

Printed and bound in April 2020 by CPI Group (UK) Ltd,
108 Beddington Lane, Croydon, CR0 4YY, United Kingdom

MIX
Paper from
responsible sources
FSC® C020471

# INTRODUCTION

Get ready to go on a problem-solving
adventure in this fun-filled book!

Take your pick of over 100 logic games. You can complete
them in any order you like and work through at your own pace.
Each puzzle gives you space to write down your answers and,
when you're finished, you can check them against the
solutions at the back.

Start each puzzle by reading the instructions. Don't worry if you
have to read the instructions a few times to be clear about what
they mean. It's a good idea to write in pencil so you can rub your
answers out if they're not quite right (and then try again!).

At the top of every page, there is a space for you to write
how much time it took you to complete the puzzle on your
first go. If you come back at a later date to try it again, you
could then see if you've got faster at it.

If you are stuck, you could try asking an adult, although did you know that your brain is actually much more powerful than a grown-up's? When you get older, your brain will get rid of lots of bits it thinks it doesn't need any more, which means you might be better at solving these games than older people are.

If you're **REALLY** stuck, have a peek at the answers at the back of the book, and then try and work out how you could have got that solution yourself.

Good luck, and have fun!

### Introducing the Logic Games Master:
### Gareth Moore, B.Sc (Hons) M.Phil Ph.D

Dr Gareth Moore is an Ace Puzzler, and author of lots of puzzle and brain-training books.

He created an online brain-training site called BrainedUp.com, and runs an online puzzle site called PuzzleMix.com. Gareth has a Ph.D from the University of Cambridge, where he taught machines to understand spoken English.

In the puzzles below, can you draw a single loop that passes through the centre of every white square, using only horizontal and vertical lines?

Take a look at this example to see how the puzzle works, then try the games below:

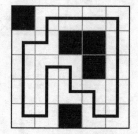

a)

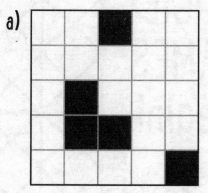

b)

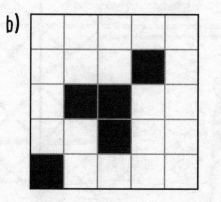

Can you draw horizontal and vertical lines to join all of the planets into pairs, so that each pair consists of one shaded and one unshaded planet? Lines cannot cross over other planets, nor each other.

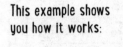

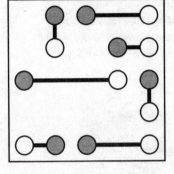

Hint: Start with the first circle on this row.

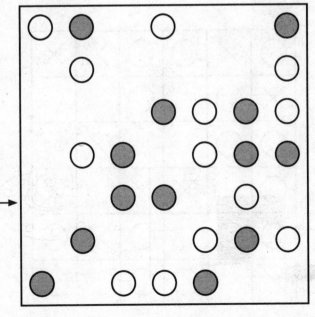

Can you help Astro Dog complete this 'no four in a row' game? Place an 'X' or an 'O' into every empty square, while making sure that you don't create any lines of four or more 'X's or 'O's in any direction, including diagonally.

Here's an example solution. Notice how there are no lines of four of the same symbol:

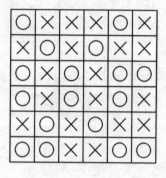

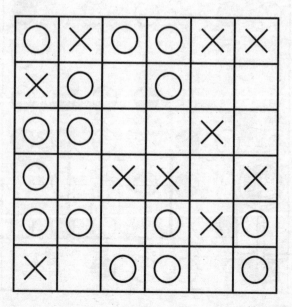

To solve each of these sudoku puzzles, place a number from 1 to 4 into every empty square so that no number repeats in any row, column or bold-lined 2x2 box.

a)

|   | 2 | 1 |   |
|---|---|---|---|
| 1 |   |   | 2 |
| 4 |   |   | 3 |
|   | 3 | 4 |   |

b)

|   |   | 1 |   |
|---|---|---|---|
|   | 1 |   |   |
|   |   | 3 |   |
|   | 4 |   |   |

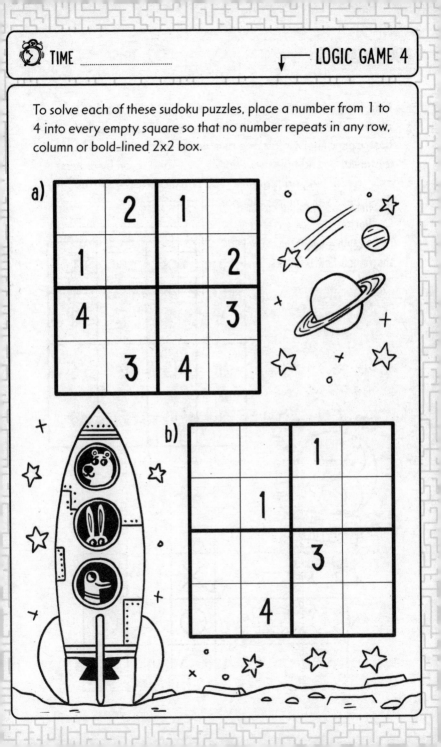

To solve the puzzles on the opposite page, fill in the empty squares so that each grid contains every number from 1 to 16 once each. There is just one rule, which is that you must be able to start at '1' and then move to '2', '3', '4' and so on by moving only to touching grid squares. You can move left, right, up or down between squares, but not diagonally.

This example solution shows you how it works:

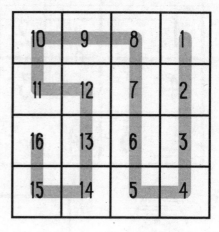

| 10 | 9  | 8 | 1 |
|----|----|---|---|
| 11 | 12 | 7 | 2 |
| 16 | 13 | 6 | 3 |
| 15 | 14 | 5 | 4 |

a)

| 11 |    |    | 16 |
|----|----|----|----|
|    | 9  | 14 |    |
|    | 8  | 1  |    |
| 6  |    |    | 3  |

b)

| 4  |    |    | 1  |
|----|----|----|----|
|    |    |    |    |
|    |    |    |    |
| 13 |    |    | 16 |

Can you join all of the dots to form a single loop that visits every dot? You can only use straight horizontal or vertical lines to join dots, and the loop can't cross or touch itself. Some parts of the loop have already been drawn in to get you started.

Here's an example solution to show you how it works:

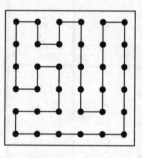

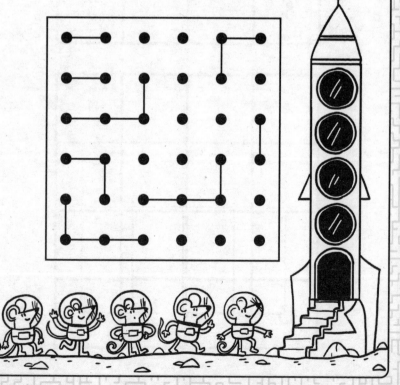

Fill in the grid by placing the letters A, B and C once each into every row and column. This means that there will be one empty square in each row and column.

The letters outside the grid show which letter appears nearest in their row or column.

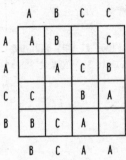

This example shows how it works:

|   | A | B | C | C |   |
|---|---|---|---|---|---|
| A | A | B |   | C | C |
| A |   | A | C | B | B |
| C | C |   | B | A | A |
| B | B | C | A |   | A |
|   | B | C | A | A |   |

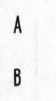

|   | B | C | A | C |   |
|---|---|---|---|---|---|
| B |   |   |   |   | C |
| C |   |   |   |   | A |
| C |   |   |   |   | B |
| A |   |   |   |   | C |
|   | A | B | C | B |   |

Can you draw a series of separate paths to connect each pair of matching space pictures together?

The paths must not cross or touch each other, and no more than one path can enter any grid square. Each path must be made up of only horizontal and vertical lines – diagonals aren't allowed.

Take a look at this example solution to see how it works:

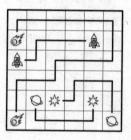

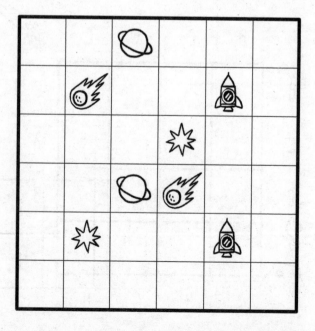

Can you use your powers of deduction to work out which of the grid squares contain hidden asteroids in these two puzzles?

- Any empty grid square can contain an asteroid, but none of the numbered squares do.
- A number in a square tells you how many asteroids there are in touching squares, including diagonally touching squares.

Here's an example solution to show you how it works:

|  | 1 | 0 |
|---|---|---|
|  |  | 1 |
|  | 3 |  |

**a)**

|  | 1 | 1 |
|---|---|---|
| 2 |  | 3 |
|  |  |  |

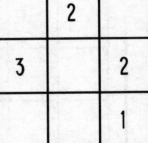

**b)**

|  | 2 |  |
|---|---|---|
| 3 |  | 2 |
|  |  | 1 |

Can you fill in this space map to reveal the rockets that are in orbit around these planets? Draw rockets in some of the empty grid squares, so each planet has exactly one rocket in a touching square to the left, right, above or below. Rockets cannot touch one another, even diagonally. The number of rockets in each row and column is shown by the numbers outside the grid.

Take a look at this example solution to see how it works:

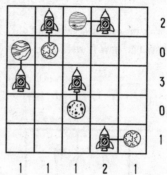

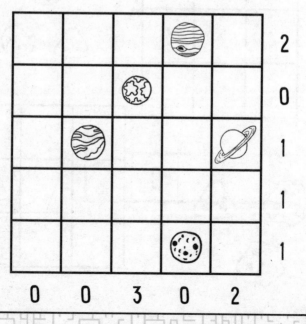

Can you help the space cat complete this grid, so that every row, column and bold-lined region contains each of the letters from A to E?

This example shows you how it works:

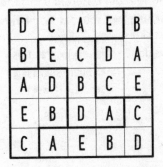

| D | C | A | E | B |
|---|---|---|---|---|
| B | E | C | D | A |
| A | D | B | C | E |
| E | B | D | A | C |
| C | A | E | B | D |

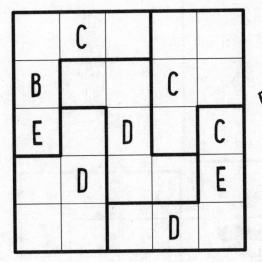

Can you place a digit from 1 to 4 into each empty square without repeating a digit within any row or column? The small digits sitting at the meeting points of some sets of four squares show the four different digits that must be found in those touching four squares. Some have been placed already.

Take a look at this example solution to see how it works:

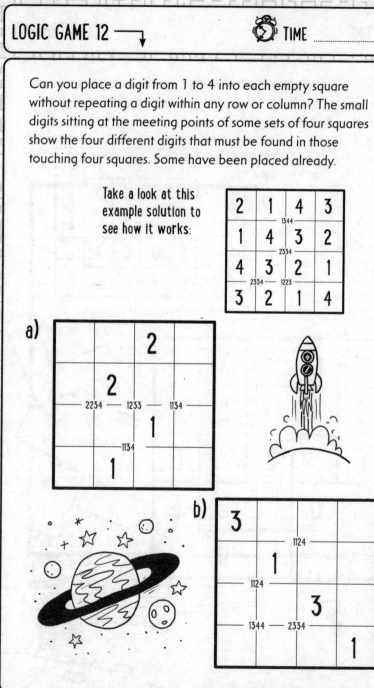

a)

b)

Put your logic skills to the test with this 'touchy' puzzle. To solve it, you need to place a letter from A to E into every empty square so that no letter repeats in any row or column.

Identical letters can't be in touching squares — not even diagonally.

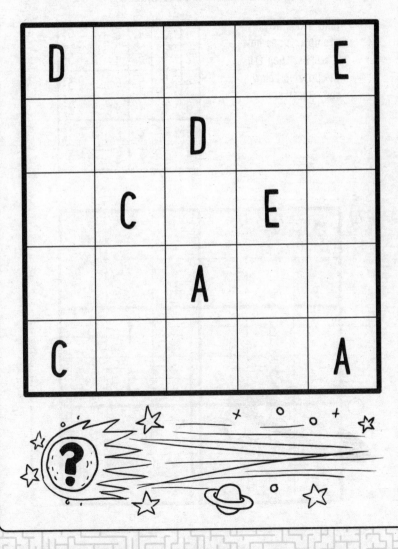

Solve these odd-even sudoku games by placing a digit from 1 to 6 into each empty unshaded or shaded square. No digit should repeat in any row, column or bold-lined 3x2 box. Also, only odd digits (1, 3, 5) can be placed in unshaded squares, and only even digits (2, 4, 6) can be placed in shaded squares.

Take a look at this example to see how it works, then try the puzzles below and opposite:

| 1 | 5 | 4 | 3 | 2 | 6 |
|---|---|---|---|---|---|
| 2 | 6 | 3 | 1 | 4 | 5 |
| 4 | 2 | 5 | 6 | 1 | 3 |
| 6 | 3 | 1 | 4 | 5 | 2 |
| 5 | 4 | 6 | 2 | 3 | 1 |
| 3 | 1 | 2 | 5 | 6 | 4 |

a)

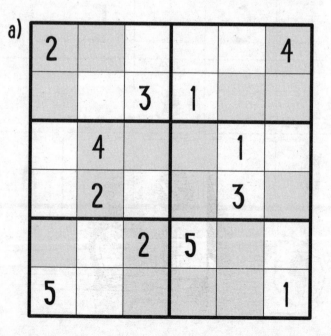

b)

| 6 |   |   |   |   | 3 |
|---|---|---|---|---|---|
|   | 3 |   |   | 4 |   |
|   |   | 6 | 1 |   |   |
|   |   | 4 | 6 |   |   |
|   | 2 |   |   | 6 |   |
| 4 |   |   |   |   | 1 |

TIME ..............

The aliens on Planet Zorg are building a new railway. Draw straight or corner railway pieces in some squares to complete the track, so it travels all the way from its entrance in the left column to its exit in the bottom row. It can't enter or exit the grid except where shown, or cross over itself. Numbers outside the grid reveal the total number of railway pieces in each row and column. Some pieces are already placed to get you started.

Take a look at this example solution to see how it works:

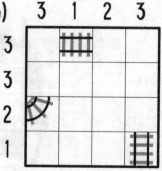

a)

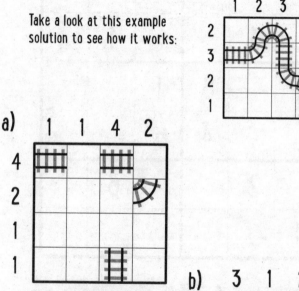

b)

Can you draw a loop that visits every square of the grid, using only horizontal and vertical lines? In each square, the loop can either pass straight through, turn or cross over itself. Apart from where it crosses over itself, it cannot enter any square more than once.

Some squares are already completed, to get you started.

This example shows you how it works:

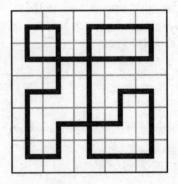

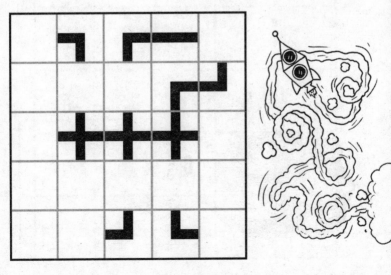

The aim of this game is to draw a single loop that travels through some, but not all, of the empty squares. The loop must visit the given number of squares next to each clue number, including diagonally touching squares. The loop can only use horizontal and vertical lines, and cannot enter any square more than once.

Take a look at the example. Notice how the loop passes through 4 squares next to the 4, through 7 squares next to the 7 and so on:

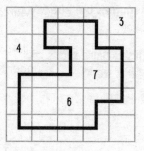

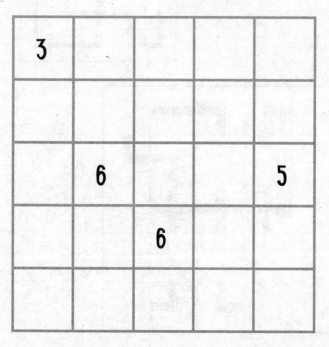

James, Marco and Selma are discussing their ages. Based on the following information, can you work out how old each astronaut animal is? (Assume that each animal's age is a whole number.)

- Selma noticed that in 3 years' time she will be twice the age that James is now.
- The total of James and Marco's ages is less than twice Selma's age.
- Marco is twice as old as James was a year ago.
- All the animals are younger than 10.

Selma is _____

James is _____

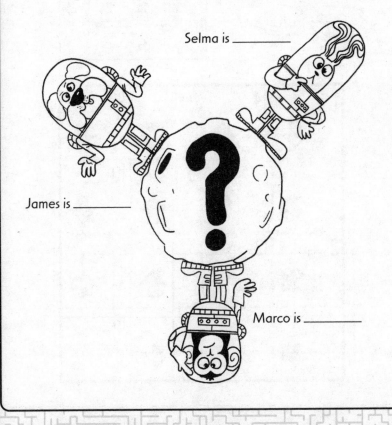

Marco is _____

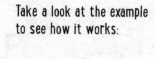
⏱ TIME ....................

This puzzle shows the path of a comet. Can you complete the grid so each number from 1 to 16 appears once, and so you can trace a path from 1 to 16 by simply following the arrows from number to number? Each arrow must point in the direction of the next number in the path.

Take a look at the example to see how it works:

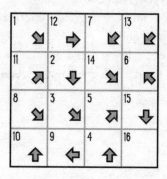

| 1 ↘ | 12 ➡ | 7 ↙ | 13 ↙ |
|---|---|---|---|
| 11 ↗ | 2 ⬇ | 14 ↘ | 6 ↖ |
| 8 ↘ | 3 ↘ | 5 ↗ | 15 ⬇ |
| 10 ⬆ | 9 ⬅ | 4 ⬆ | 16 |

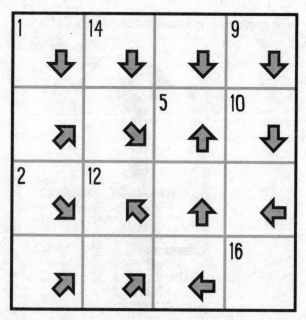

| 1 ⬇ | 14 ⬇ | ⬇ | 9 ⬇ |
|---|---|---|---|
| ↗ | ↘ | 5 ⬆ | 10 ⬇ |
| 2 ↘ | 12 ↖ | ⬆ | ⬅ |
| ↗ | ↗ | 16 ⬅ | |

Can you draw along some of the dashed lines to divide this map of a space station into four identical sections, with no unused squares left over?

Each of the four sections must be identical, although they can be rotated versions of each other.

This example shows how it works:

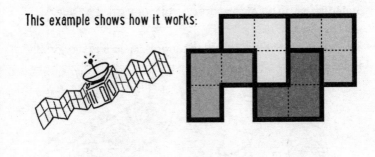

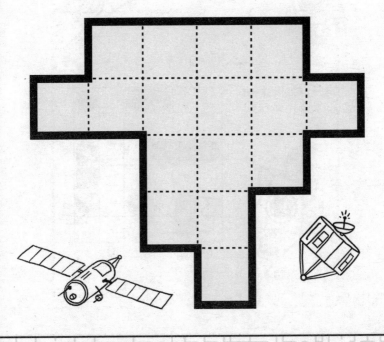

Complete the spaceship puzzle on the opposite page by placing the given set of spaceships into the grid. The spaceships are of three different lengths, with two spaceships of each length.

- Each row and column has a number next to it. This tells you how many squares in that row or column contain part of a spaceship.
- Spaceships can be placed horizontally or vertically, but not diagonally.
- Spaceships can't be in touching squares, including diagonally touching squares.

This example shows you how it works:

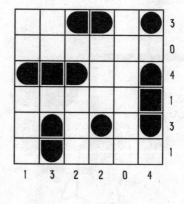

Now try the puzzle below. Four spaceship parts have already
been placed to get you started.

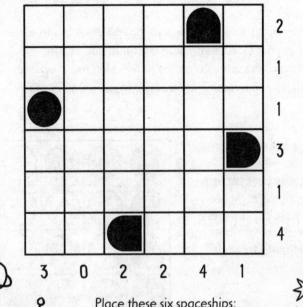

2
1
1
3
1
4

3 0 2 2 4 1

Place these six spaceships:

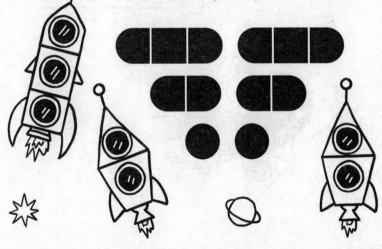

Help this alien solve each of these puzzles by placing either a shaded or an unshaded circle into every empty square, so that there are no 2x2 (or larger) areas of circles of the same colour.

You must also place the circles so that all those of the same colour connect together. This means that you can travel to any circle of the same colour by moving left, right, up and down between touching squares of the same colour of circle.

Take a look at this example solution, which also shows the connections between touching circles. Notice how there are two areas – one of shaded circles and one of unshaded circles:

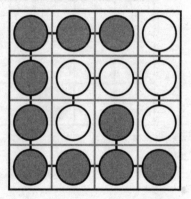

a)

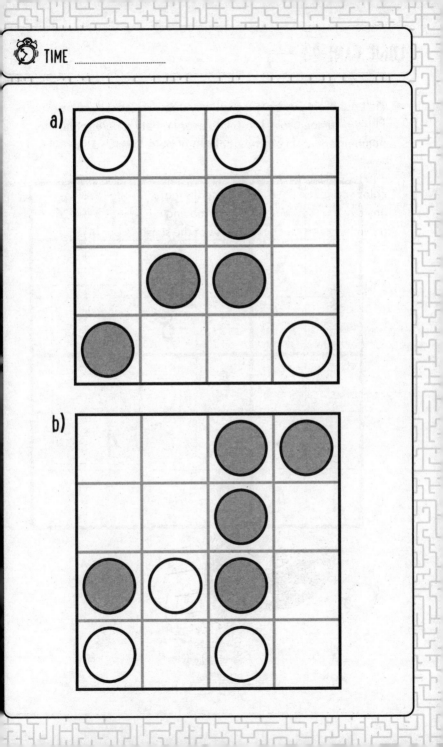

b)

Put your brain power to the test with these mega sudoku puzzles. Place a number from 1 to 6 into every empty square so that no number repeats in any row, column or bold-lined 2x3 box.

a)

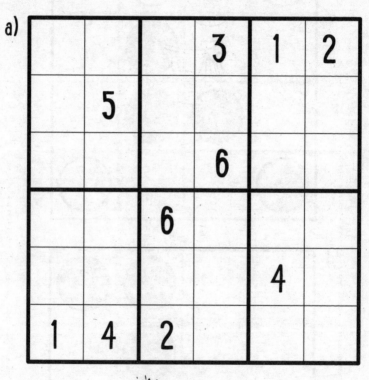

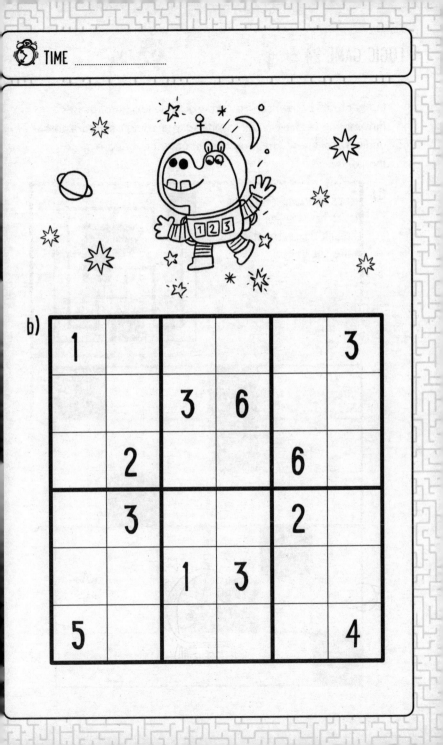

**b)**

| 1 |   |   |   |   | 3 |
|---|---|---|---|---|---|
|   |   | 3 | 6 |   |   |
|   | 2 |   |   | 6 |   |
|   | 3 |   |   | 2 |   |
|   |   | 1 | 3 |   |   |
| 5 |   |   |   |   | 4 |

⏱ TIME ...................

In the puzzle below, can you draw a single loop that passes through the centre of every white square, using only horizontal and vertical lines? The loop cannot enter any square more than once.

Here's an example solution. Notice how the line passes through the centre of every white square:

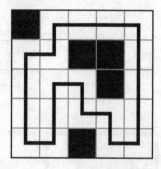

Shade some squares in the image below to reveal a hidden pattern. The numbers reveal how many shaded squares there are in each row or column, reading from left to right or top to bottom.

- If there is just one number then this tells you that there are that many touching shaded squares in the row or column, and the rest of the row or column is empty.
- If there are multiple numbers then there are as many sets of shaded squares as there are numbers, with each set being of the length shown — and in the order given.

For example, if a clue was '2, 1' then there would be two shaded squares, a gap of one or more empty squares, and then one shaded square — and the rest of the row or column would be empty.

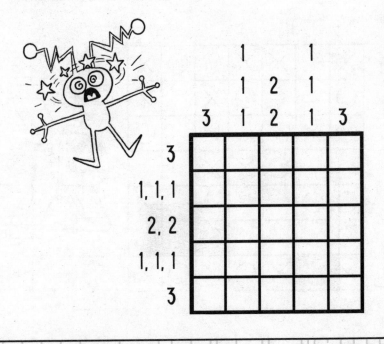

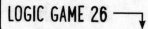
Can you help the astro-animals complete this 'no four in a row' game? Place an 'X' or an 'O' into every empty square, while making sure that you don't create any lines of four or more 'X's or 'O's in any direction, including diagonally.

**This example shows how it works:**

| O | X | X | X | O | X |
|---|---|---|---|---|---|
| X | O | X | O | X | X |
| O | X | O | X | O | O |
| O | X | O | X | O | X |
| O | X | O | X | X | X |
| O | O | X | X | O | O |

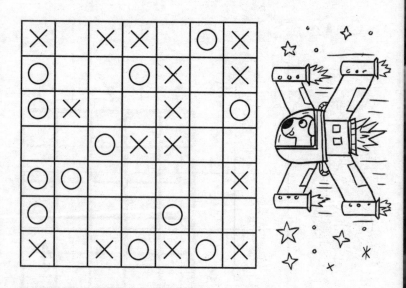

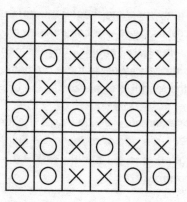

Shade in some squares to make a pattern. Each number shows the total number of touching squares – including diagonally touching squares and the square with the number in – that must be shaded.

Take a look at the numbers in this completed example. Notice how they match the number of surrounding shaded squares:

| | | 2 | | 3 |
|---|---|---|---|---|
| 3 | 4 | | | |
| 2 | | 1 | 3 | |
| 3 | | | 5 | |
| | 4 | 3 | | 3 |

| 4 | 4 | | | 4 |
|---|---|---|---|---|
| | | | | 4 |
| | | 5 | | |
| 4 | | | | |
| 4 | | | 4 | 4 |

The aim of this puzzle is to draw lines representing rocket flightpaths between the planets.

- Each planet contains a number. Each planet must have the same number of flightpaths connected to it as that number.
- Flightpaths can't cross over other flightpaths or planets.
- There can be no more than two flightpaths between any pair of planets.
- Only horizontal and vertical flightpaths are allowed.

You must arrange the set of flightpaths so that someone could fly from one planet to any other planet, just by using the flightpaths that you've drawn.

This example shows you how it works:

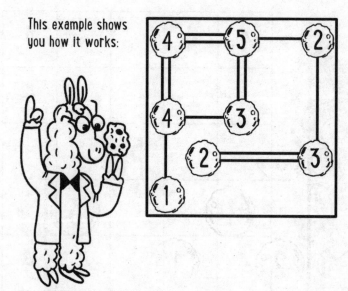

TIME ..............................................

a)

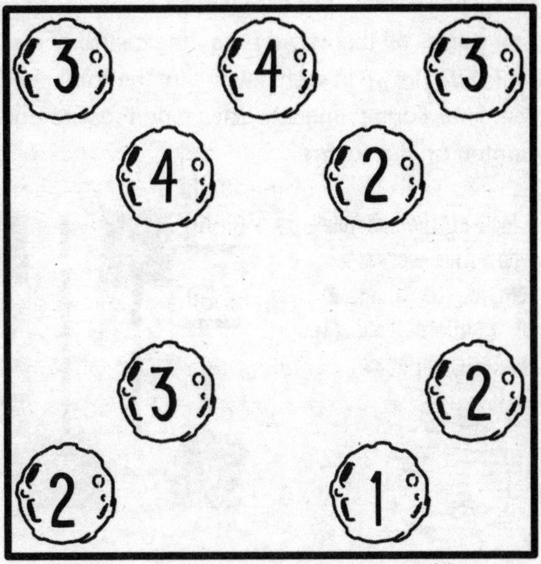
3 4 3
4 2
3 2
2 1

b)

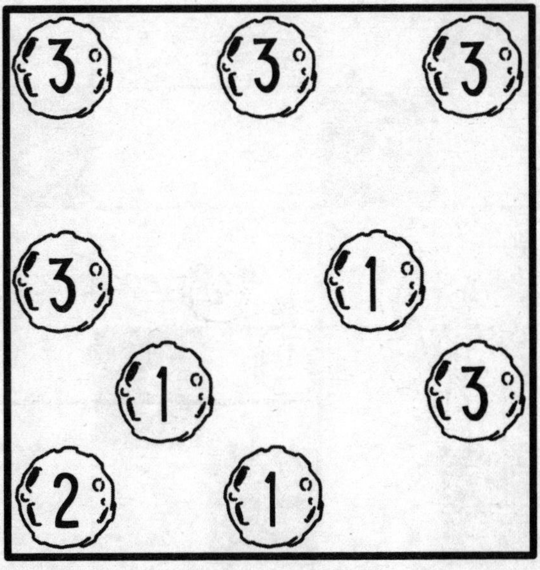
3 3 3
3 1
1 3
2 1

Draw either a horizontal or vertical line in each empty square, so that the line passes all the way through the centre of the square. The lines must be drawn in such a way that the total number of squares with lines connecting to each shaded square equals the number printed on the square.

Take a look at the example to see how this works. For example, the '5' has a total of 5 squares connected to it via touching lines:

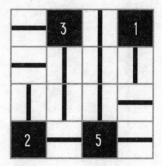

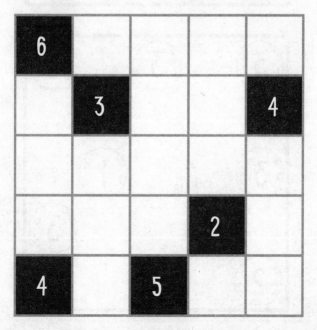

To solve this puzzle, draw along the dashed lines to divide the grid into a set of rectangles and squares, so that each shape contains exactly one number. Each number must be equal to the number of grid squares contained within that shape.

Take a look at this solved example:

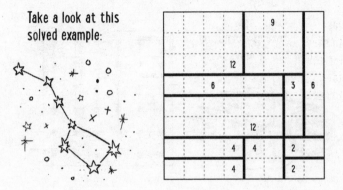

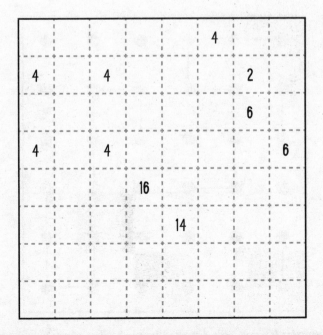

Can you join all of the dots to form a single loop that visits every dot? You can only use straight horizontal or vertical lines to join dots, and the loop can't cross or touch itself. Some parts of the loop have already been drawn in to get you started.

Here's an example solution to show how it works:

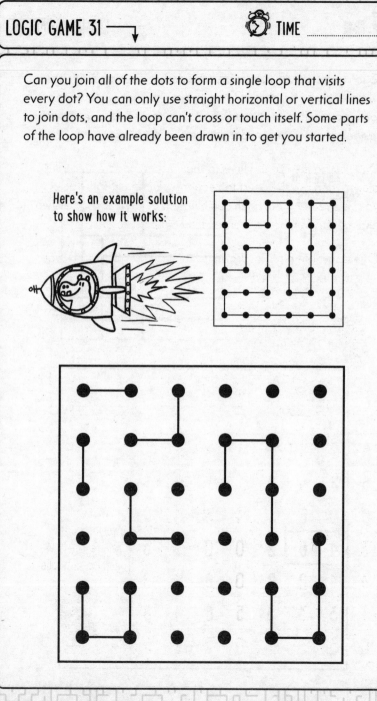

Can you help Astro Cat work out how to fit a complete set of dominoes into the grid? The number of spots on the end of each domino is given, but it's up to you to join them into pairs representing the actual domino tiles.

Draw along the dashed lines to show where each domino is placed, and use the chart to keep track of which dominoes you've already used. Each combination of numbers on the two ends of the domino appears exactly once in the grid.

One domino is already drawn in and marked off, to show you how it works.

| 0 | 1 | 2 | 3 | 4 | 5 | 6 |   |
|---|---|---|---|---|---|---|---|
|   |   |   |   |   |   |   | 0 |
|   |   |   |   |   |   |   | 1 |
|   |   |   |   |   |   |   | 2 |
|   |   |   |   |   |   |   | 3 |
|   |   |   |   |   | ✓ |   | 4 |
|   |   |   |   |   |   |   | 5 |
|   |   |   |   |   |   |   | 6 |

| 6 | 2 | 4 | 5 | 1 | 5 | 5 | 1 |
|---|---|---|---|---|---|---|---|
| 6 | 5 | 5 | 2 | 1 | 1 | 0 | 4 |
| 5 | 0 | 0 | 3 | 4 | 3 | 4 | 6 |
| 3 | 4 | 6 | 2 | 0 | 0 | 5 | 3 |
| 4 | 4 | 2 | 2 | 0 | 6 | 6 | 2 |
| 1 | 3 | 3 | 3 | 5 | 6 | 4 | 6 |
| 0 | 3 | 1 | 1 | 0 | 2 | 2 | 1 |

Hint: Start by working out where the '4 4' domino must go.

Place a digit from 1 to 6 into each square that does not already contain a digit, so no digit repeats in any row, column or 3x2 box. The puzzle contains three space worms. The digits placed along the body of each space worm must increase by 1 at each step along the body of the worm, from its tail to its head. Take a look at the example solution, and notice how the numbers written along the worms obey this rule: they are '456', '1234' and '234'.

Here's an example
solution:

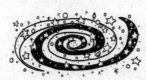

| 5 | 2 | 3 | 1 | 6 | 4 |
|---|---|---|---|---|---|
| 6 | 1 | 4 | 2 | 5 | 3 |
| 3 | 5 | 2 | 4 | 1 | 6 |
| 4 | 6 | 1 | 3 | 2 | 5 |
| 1 | 3 | 6 | 5 | 4 | 2 |
| 2 | 4 | 5 | 6 | 3 | 1 |

Hint: Start by working out which numbers must be placed on the worms. You can place all of these first.

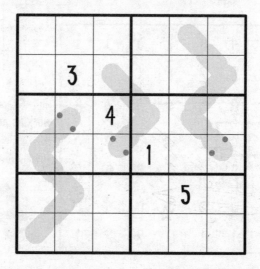

A team of space mice are building a railway on Planet Zyborg. Draw straight or corner railway pieces in some squares in order to complete the track, so it travels all the way from its entrance in the left column to its exit in the bottom row. It can't enter or exit the grid except where shown, or cross over itself. Numbers outside the grid reveal the total number of railway pieces in each row and column. Some pieces are already placed to get you started.

Take a look at this example to see how it works, then try these two puzzles:

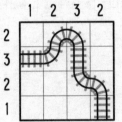

**a)**

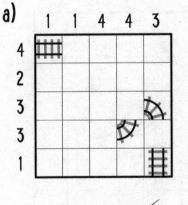

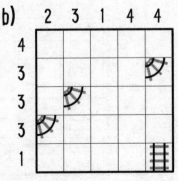

**b)**

Can you draw a series of separate paths to connect each pair of identical space shapes together? The paths must not cross or touch each other, and no more than one path can enter any grid square. Each path must be made up of only horizontal and vertical lines — diagonals aren't allowed.

Take a look at the example solution to see how it works:

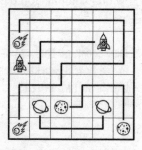

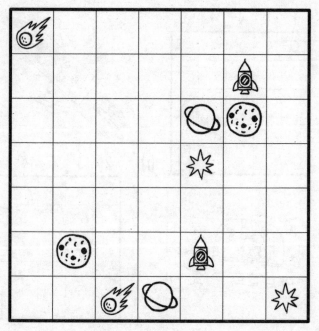

Can you fill in the empty squares so that the grid contains every number from 1 to 25 once each? There is just one rule, which is that you must be able to start at '1' and then move to '2', '3', '4' and so on by moving only to touching grid squares. You can move left, right, up and down between squares, but not diagonally.

Here's an example solution to show you how it works:

| 1 | 6 | 7 | 14 | 15 |
| 2 | 5 | 8 | 13 | 16 |
| 3 | 4 | 9 | 12 | 17 |
| 24 | 23 | 10 | 11 | 18 |
| 25 | 22 | 21 | 20 | 19 |

| 21 |    | 23 |    | 25 |
|----|----|----|----|----|
|    | 17 |    | 15 |    |
| 19 |    | 1  |    | 13 |
|    | 3  |    | 11 |    |
| 5  |    | 7  |    | 9  |

⏱ TIME ............................

To solve each of these sudoku puzzles, place a number from 1 to 6 into every empty square so that no number repeats in any row, column or bold-lined 2x3 box.

**a)**

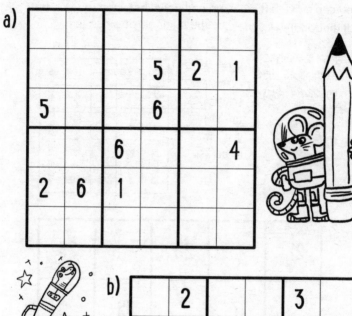

|   |   |   |   |   |   |
|---|---|---|---|---|---|
|   |   |   |   |   |   |
|   |   |   | 5 | 2 | 1 |
| 5 |   |   | 6 |   |   |
|   |   | 6 |   |   | 4 |
| 2 | 6 | 1 |   |   |   |
|   |   |   |   |   |   |

**b)**

|   | 2 |   |   | 3 |   |
|---|---|---|---|---|---|
| 6 |   |   |   |   | 1 |
|   |   | 1 | 4 |   |   |
|   |   | 5 | 6 |   |   |
| 2 |   |   |   |   | 5 |
|   | 5 |   |   | 6 |   |

Can you fill in this space map to reveal the rockets that are in orbit around these planets? Draw rockets in some of the empty grid squares, so each planet has exactly one rocket in a touching square to the left, right, above or below. Rockets cannot touch one another, even diagonally. The number of rockets in each row and column is shown by the numbers outside the grid.

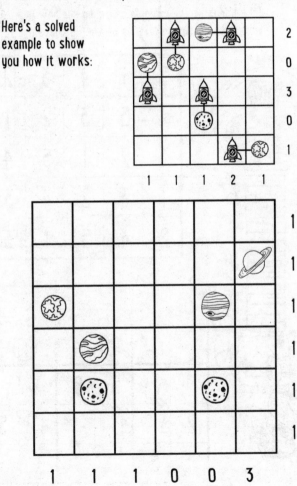

Here's a solved example to show you how it works:

Can you place a digit from 1 to 5 into each empty square without repeating a digit within any row or column? The small digits that sit at the meeting points of some sets of four squares show the four different digits that must be found in those touching four squares. Some have been placed already.

Take a look at the example below to see how it works, then try the puzzles on the opposite page:

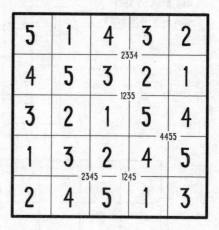

| 5 | 1 | 4 | 3 | 2 |
|---|---|---|---|---|
| 4 | 5 | 3 | 2 | 1 |
| 3 | 2 | 1 | 5 | 4 |
| 1 | 3 | 2 | 4 | 5 |
| 2 | 4 | 5 | 1 | 3 |

2334
1235
4455
2345 — 1245

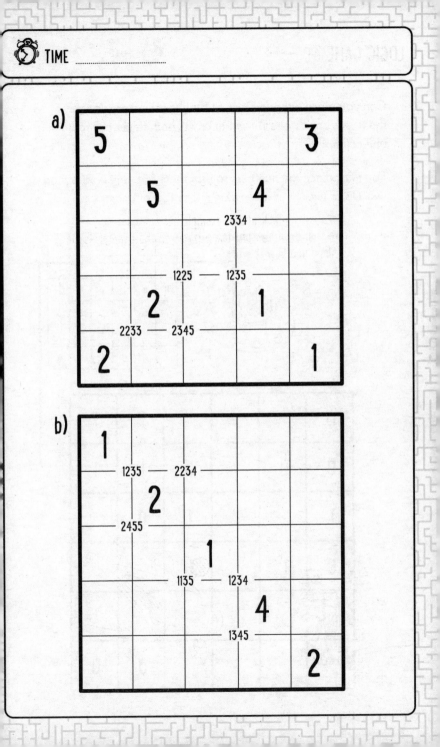

Can you place either a '0' or a '1' into each empty square so that there are an equal number of '0's and '1's in each row and column?

You must place the numbers so that there are never more than two '0's or two '1's in succession in any row or column.

**Here's an example solution to show you how it works:**

| 1 | 1 | 0 | 0 | 1 | 0 |
|---|---|---|---|---|---|
| 0 | 0 | 1 | 0 | 1 | 1 |
| 0 | 0 | 1 | 1 | 0 | 1 |
| 1 | 1 | 0 | 0 | 1 | 0 |
| 0 | 0 | 1 | 1 | 0 | 1 |
| 1 | 1 | 0 | 1 | 0 | 0 |

| 0 |   |   |   | 1 | 1 |
|---|---|---|---|---|---|
| 0 | 0 |   | 0 | 1 | 1 |
| 1 |   | 1 | 1 | 0 |   |
| 0 | 1 |   | 0 |   |   |
|   |   | 1 |   |   |   |
|   |   |   |   | 0 | 0 |

Draw a loop showing the route of a spaceship as it visits every square of the grid, using only horizontal and vertical lines. In each square, the loop can either pass straight through, turn or cross over itself. Apart from where it crosses over itself, it cannot enter any square more than once. Some squares are already completed, to get you started.

**Take a look at the example solution to see how it works:**

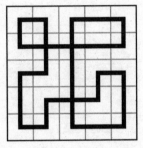

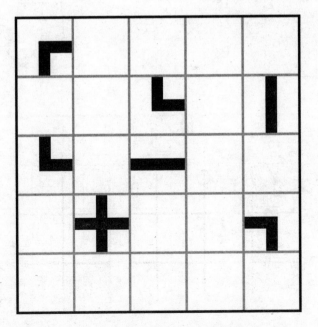

⏰ TIME ........................

Can you solve these futoshiki puzzles by placing the numbers 1 to 4 once each into every row and column? You must obey the arrows, which act as 'greater than' signs. The arrows always point from the bigger number to the smaller number of a pair. This means that, for example, you could have '2 > 1' since 2 is greater than 1, but '1 > 2' would be wrong because 1 is not greater in value than 2.

a)

b)

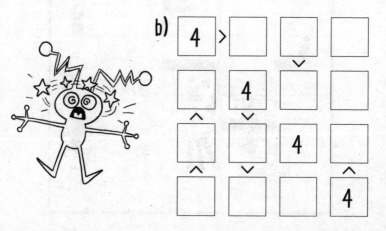

Shivani, Luis and Isabella are all drawing three different sketches, and they are each using a different pen. Based on the following information, can you work out the type of pen each animal is using, and what each one is drawing?

1. The ballpoint pen is not being used by Luis.

2. The person drawing the astronaut is not using the fountain pen.

3. The moonscape is not being drawn using a felt pen.

4. Shivani is not drawing a rocket.

5. The rocket is being drawn with a ballpoint pen.

6. Luis is not drawing the moonscape.

Can you use your powers of deduction to work out which of the grid squares contain hidden asteroids in this puzzle?

- Any empty grid square can contain an asteroid, but none of the numbered squares do.
- A number in a square tells you how many asteroids there are in touching squares, including diagonally touching squares.

Take a look at this example solution to see how it works:

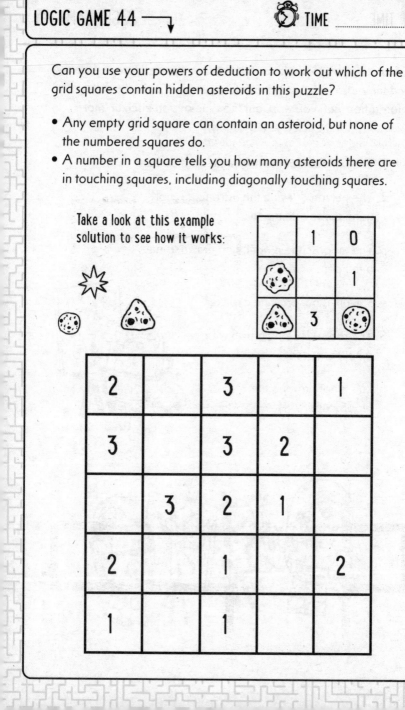

Can you draw along some of the dashed lines on this map of a space station to divide it into four identical pieces, with no unused parts left over?

Each of the four pieces must be identical, although they can be rotated versions of each other.

This example shows you how it works:

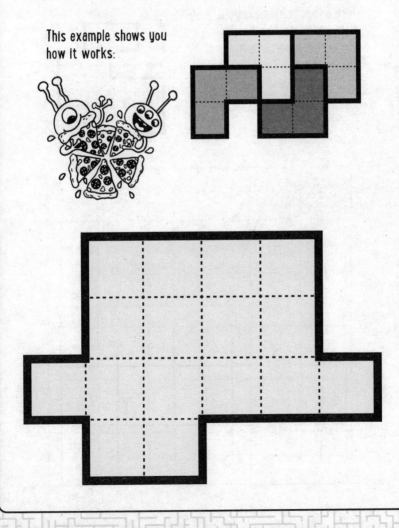

Draw a single loop that travels through some, but not all, of the white squares. The loop must visit the given number of squares next to each clue number, including diagonally touching squares. The loop can only use horizontal and vertical lines, and cannot enter any square more than once.

Take a look at this example. Notice how the loop passes through 4 squares next to the 4, through 7 squares next to the 7 and so on:

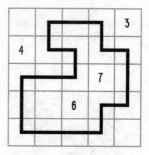

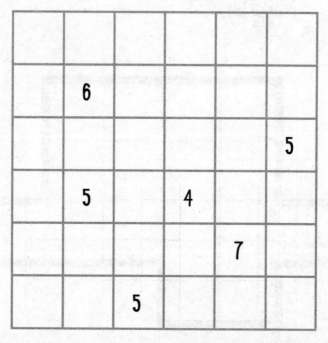

Can you fill in this space map to reveal the rockets that are in orbit around these planets? Draw rockets in some of the empty grid squares, so each planet has exactly one rocket in a touching square to the left, right, above or below. Rockets cannot touch one another, even diagonally. The number of rockets in each row and column is shown by the numbers outside the grid.

Take a look at the example solution to see how it works:

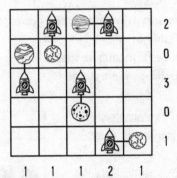

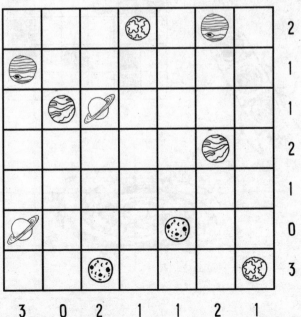

Can you complete the spaceship puzzle on the opposite page by placing the given set of spaceships into the grid? The spaceships are of three different lengths, with two spaceships of each length.

- Each row and column has a number next to it. This tells you how many squares in that row or column contain part of a spaceship.
- Spaceships can be placed horizontally or vertically, but not diagonally.
- Spaceships can't be in touching squares, including diagonally touching squares.

This example shows you how it works:

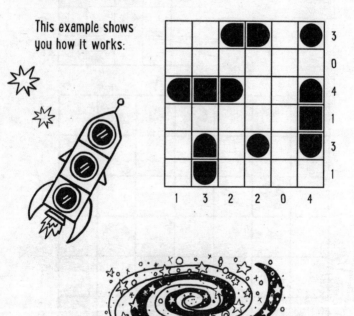

In the puzzle below, two spaceship parts are already placed to get you started, as well as a square marked with a planet to show that it doesn't contain part of a ship.

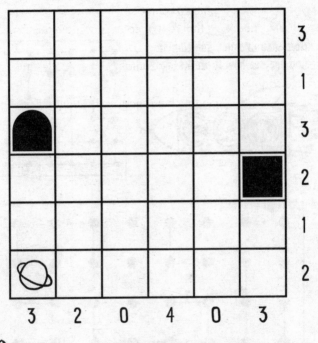

Place these six spaceships:

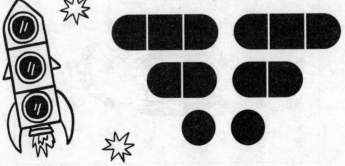

Can you join all of the dots to form a single loop that visits every dot? You can only use straight horizontal or vertical lines to join dots, and the loop can't cross or touch itself. Some parts of the loop have already been drawn in to get you started.

Here's an example solution so you can see how it works:

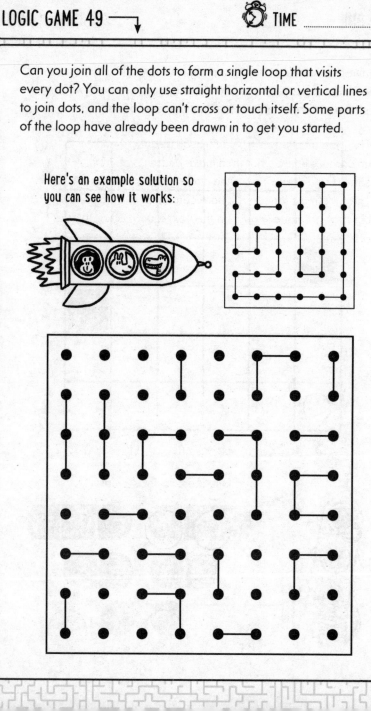

Draw a loop that passes through some of the squares, made up of horizontal and vertical lines. The loop must visit every square containing a circle, and cannot enter any square more than once.

- The loop must pass straight through a square containing an unshaded circle but then make a turn in the next square either as it enters or exits the circle – or both.
- The loop must turn on a square containing a shaded circle, but then continue straight in the next square on both sides of the circle.

Take a look at the example to see how it works. Notice how the unshaded and shaded circles follow the rules given above:

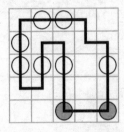

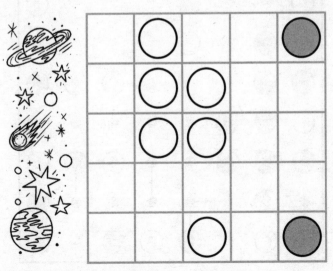

Draw horizontal and vertical lines to join all of the planets into pairs, so that each pair consists of one unshaded and one shaded planet. Lines cannot cross over other planets, or each other.

Here's an example solution to show you how it works:

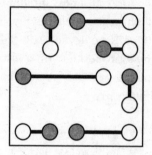

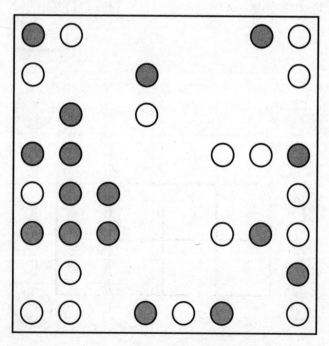

Fill in the grid by placing the letters A, B and C once each into every row and column. This means that there will be one empty square in each row and column.

The letters outside the grid show which letter appears nearest in their row or column.

Take a look at this example to see how it works:

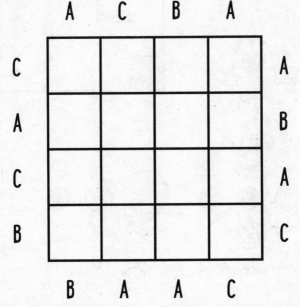

Can you complete the path puzzles on the opposite page? You need to join some of the dots in order to draw a path that travels from one black dot to the other. The exact number of dots visited in each row and column is given, and the path can only travel horizontally or vertically between dots.

The path cannot cross over any of the shaded squares, and nor can it cross over itself or use a dot more than once.

This example shows you how it works:

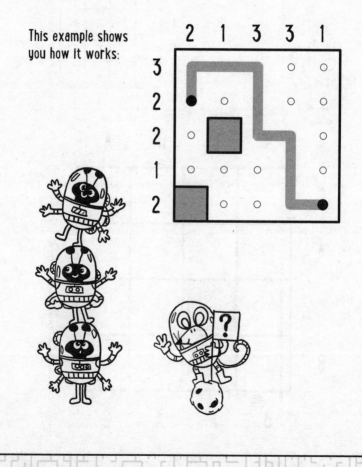

a)

|   | 1 | 1 | 2 | 5 | 2 |
|---|---|---|---|---|---|
| 2 | ○ | ▓ | ○ | ○ | ▓ |
| 5 | ● | ○ | ○ | ○ | ○ |
| 2 | ○ | ○ | ○ | ○ | ○ |
| 1 | ○ | ○ | ○ | ○ | ○ |
| 1 | ○ | ○ | ▓ | ● | ○ |

b)

|   | 1 | 2 | 3 | 3 | 2 |
|---|---|---|---|---|---|
| 1 | ○ | ○ | ○ | ▓ | ● |
| 3 | ○ | ○ | ○ | ○ | ○ |
| 2 | ○ | ▓ | ○ | ○ | ▓ |
| 3 | ○ | ○ | ○ | ○ | ○ |
| 2 | ● | ○ | ○ | ○ | ○ |

The aim of this puzzle is to draw lines representing rocket flightpaths between the planets.

- Each planet contains a number. Each planet must have the same number of flightpaths connected to it as that number.
- Planets can't cross over other flightpaths or planets.
- There can be no more than two flightpaths between any pair of planets.
- Only horizontal and vertical flightpaths are allowed.

You must arrange the set of flightpaths so that someone could fly from one planet to any other planet, just by using the flightpaths that you've drawn.

Here's an example solution to show you how it works:

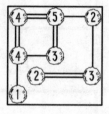

Shade some squares in the image below to reveal a hidden pattern. The numbers reveal how many shaded squares there are in each row or column, reading from left to right or top to bottom.

- If there is just one number then this tells you that there are that many touching shaded squares in the row or column, and the rest of the row or column is empty.
- If there are multiple numbers then there are as many sets of shaded squares as there are numbers, with each set being of the length shown – and in the order given.

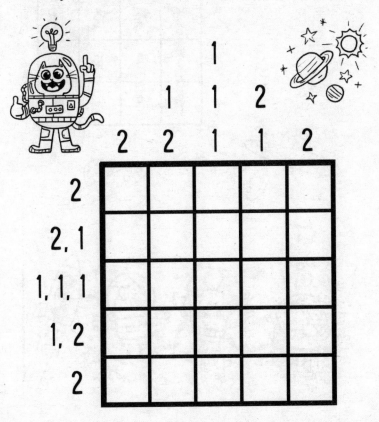

Can you fill in the empty squares in the puzzles on the opposite page so that each grid contains every number from 1 to 16?

There is just one rule, which is that you must be able to start at '1' and then move to '2', '3', '4' and so on by moving only to touching grid squares, including diagonally touching squares.

Take a look at this
example solution to
see how it works:

| 3 | 4 | 1 | 13 |
|---|---|---|---|
| 5 | 2 | 12 | 14 |
| 6 | 9 | 15 | 11 |
| 7 | 8 | 10 | 16 |

a)

|    |    | 16 | 11 |
|----|----|----|----|
| 2  | 15 |    | 10 |
| 1  |    | 7  | 9  |
| 4  | 5  |    | 8  |

b)

|    | 1  | 11 |    |
|----|----|----|----|
| 2  |    | 9  | 12 |
| 5  |    | 13 | 14 |
| 7  |    | 15 | 16 |

Draw a loop showing the path of a rocket as it visits every white square, travelling horizontally or vertically between touching squares. The loop cannot enter any square more than once.

Take a look at this example solution to see how it works:

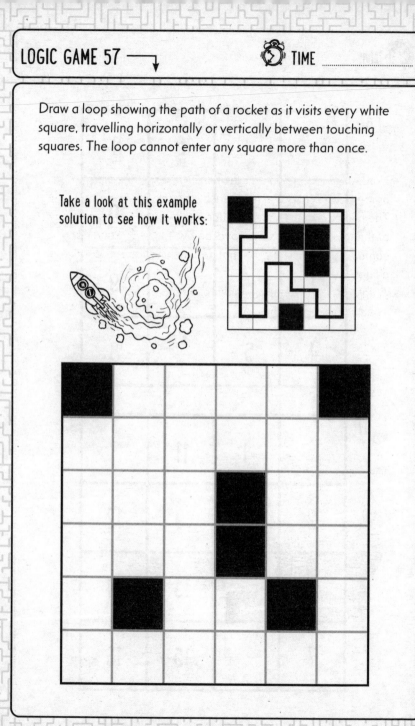

The aim of this puzzle is to place lights into some of the empty grid squares so that every empty white square is lit by at least one light.

- Lights shine along grid squares in the same row or column as far as the first black square they reach. They don't shine diagonally.
- The numbers in the shaded squares tell you exactly how many of the touching squares (above, below, to the left and right) contain lights. A '0' means that no touching squares contain a light.
- A light isn't allowed to shine directly on any other light.
- You can place lights on any empty square so long as the rules are followed – they don't have to be next to the number clues.

Take a look at this example solution. Notice how each white square is lit up by at least one light:

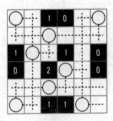

Are you ready for a challenge? The puzzle on the opposite page is made up of three overlapping 6x6 sudoku grids, which must all be solved at the same time to reach the final answer. Each of the three grids is outlined with a lighter border. See puzzles 23 or 37 for instructions on solving 6x6 sudoku puzzles. If you haven't solved either of those puzzles yet, it's a good idea to try at least one of them before tackling this game.

Here's an example solution to show you how this puzzle works:

| 5 | 4 | 2 | 1 | 6 | 3 |   |   |   |   |   |   |
|---|---|---|---|---|---|---|---|---|---|---|---|
| 2 | 3 | 6 | 5 | 1 | 4 |   |   |   |   |   |   |
| 6 | 1 | 4 | 3 | 2 | 5 |   |   |   |   |   |   |
| 3 | 5 | 1 | 2 | 4 | 6 | 3 | 5 |   |   |   |   |
| 4 | 2 | 5 | 6 | 3 | 1 | 2 | 4 |   |   |   |   |
| 1 | 6 | 3 | 4 | 5 | 2 | 6 | 1 |   |   |   |   |
|   |   | 2 | 1 | 6 | 4 | 5 | 3 | 2 | 1 |   |   |
|   |   | 6 | 3 | 1 | 5 | 4 | 2 | 6 | 3 |   |   |
|   |   | 4 | 5 | 2 | 3 | 1 | 6 | 5 | 4 |   |   |
|   |   |   |   | 5 | 6 | 3 | 4 | 1 | 2 |   |   |
|   |   |   |   | 3 | 2 | 6 | 1 | 4 | 5 |   |   |
|   |   |   |   | 4 | 1 | 2 | 5 | 3 | 6 |   |   |

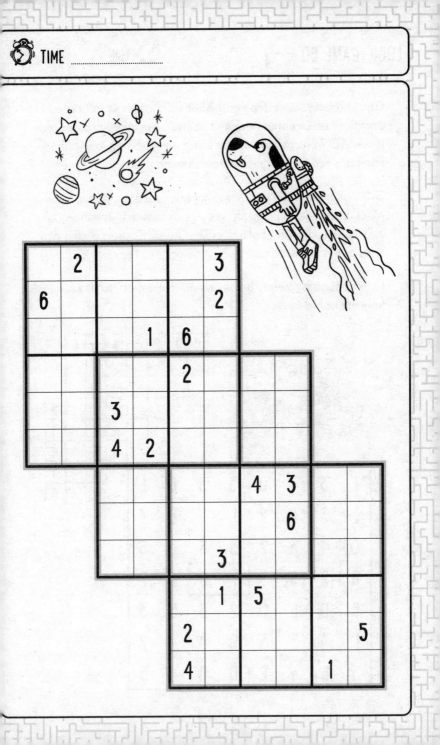

TIME ................................

Can you help Space Dog and Alien work out how to fit a complete set of dominoes into the grid? The number of spots on the end of each domino is given, but it's up to you to join them into pairs representing the actual domino tiles.

Draw along the dashed lines to show where each domino is placed, and use the chart to keep track of which dominoes you've already used. Each combination of numbers on the two ends of the domino appears exactly once in the grid.

One domino is already drawn in and marked off, to show you how the game works.

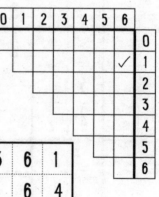

| 1 | 3 | 4 | 0 | 3 | 3 | 6 | 1 |
| 1 | 5 | 6 | 2 | 1 | 1 | 6 | 4 |
| 0 | 4 | 3 | 2 | 5 | 5 | 1 | 5 |
| 6 | 2 | 3 | 3 | 1 | 6 | 2 | 2 |
| 6 | 0 | 6 | 0 | 2 | 0 | 5 | 3 |
| 1 | 4 | 5 | 3 | 0 | 4 | 4 | 2 |
| 5 | 6 | 4 | 2 | 0 | 0 | 4 | 5 |

Place a letter from A to E into each empty square in the grid below, so that no letter repeats in any row or column.

Identical letters can't be in touching squares — not even diagonally.

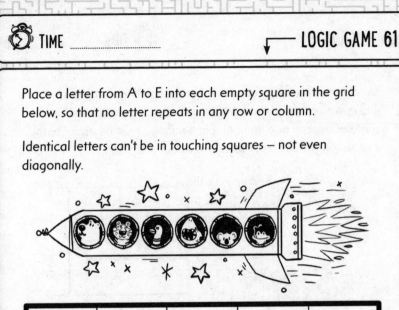

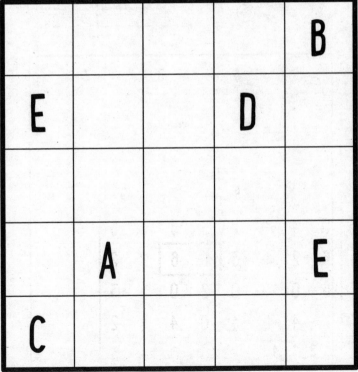

To solve this puzzle, draw along the dashed lines to divide the grid into a set of rectangles and squares, so that each shape contains exactly one number. Each number must be equal to the number of grid squares contained within that shape.

Here's an example solution to show you how it works:

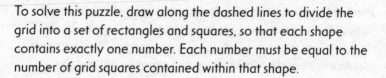

These astronauts are travelling around the Planet Zipton by train. Draw straight or corner railway pieces in some squares to complete the track, so it travels all the way from its entrance in the left column to its exit in the bottom row. It can't enter or exit the grid except where shown, or cross over itself. Numbers outside the grid reveal the total number of railway pieces in each row and column. Some pieces are already placed to get you started.

Take a look at this example to see how it works:

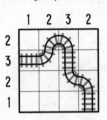

**a)**

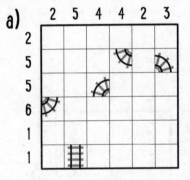

**b)**

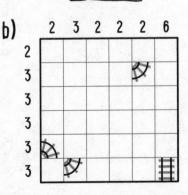

Place a digit from 1 to 3 into each square so that no digit repeats in any row or column.

Each digit represents an alien building of that many floors, and the numbers outside the grid reveal the total number of alien buildings that can be 'seen' from the point of view of that number. Taller buildings obscure shorter buildings, but never the other way around.

For example, a clue of '3' must mean that the digits reading away from that number are '1 2 3', in that order, so that all three alien buildings can be seen. On the other hand, a clue of '1' means that the digit next to that number must be a '3', since only one alien building can be seen and so it must be the tallest building.

Take a look at the example to see how this works:

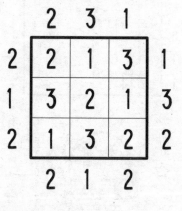

```
      2  3  1
   2  2  1  3  1
   1  3  2  1  3
   2  1  3  2  2
      2  1  2
```

**a)**

|     | 3 | 1 | 2 |     |
|-----|---|---|---|-----|
| 2   |   |   |   | 2   |
| 2   |   |   |   | 1   |
| 1   |   |   |   | 3   |
|     | 1 | 2 | 2 |     |

**b)**

|     | 1 | 3 | 2 |     |
|-----|---|---|---|-----|
| 1   |   |   |   | 2   |
| 3   |   |   |   | 1   |
| 2   |   |   |   | 2   |
|     | 2 | 1 | 2 |     |

This puzzle is called a 'killer sudoku' because it's a much trickier version of regular sudoku! Not only must you place 1 to 4 once each into every row, column and bold-lined 2x2 box, but you must also solve all of the 'killer clues'.

Each 'killer clue' consists of a number at the top-left of a dashed-line region of grid squares. All the numbers you place in that region must add up to the small number printed in the top left-hand corner of that region. Not only that, but you can't repeat the same number within any dashed-line region.

Take a look at the example solution to see how it works:

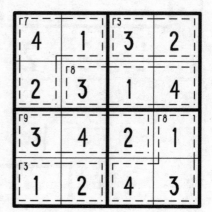

a)

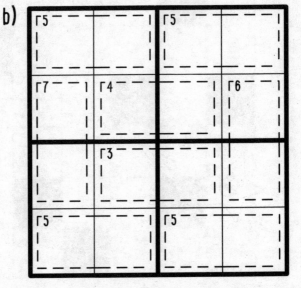

b)

⏱ TIME ........................................

Draw either a horizontal or vertical line in each empty square, so that the line passes all the way through the centre of the square. The lines must be drawn in such a way that the total number of squares with lines connecting to each shaded square equals the number printed on the square.

Take a look at the example to see how this works. For example, the '5' has a total of 5 squares connected to it via touching lines:

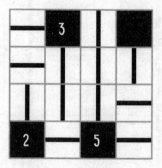

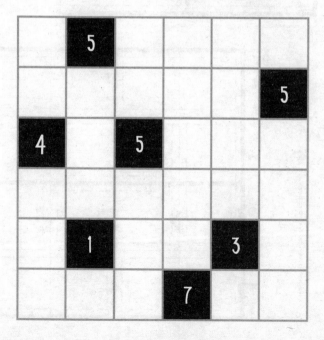

Can you solve this grid so each number from 1 to 16 appears once, and so that you can trace a path for Space Mouse from 1 through to 16 simply by following the arrows from number to number? Each arrow must point in the direction of the next number in the path.

This example shows you how it works:

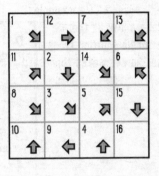

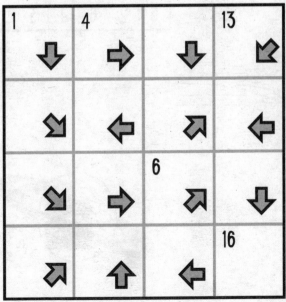

To solve the puzzles on the opposite page, can you place a digit from 1 to 6 into each empty square without repeating a digit within any row or column? The small digits that sit at the meeting points of some sets of four squares show the four different digits that must be found in those four touching squares. Some have been placed already.

Take a look at the example solution to see how it works:

| 6 | 4 | 5 | 3 | 1 | 2 |
|---|---|---|---|---|---|
| 2 | 6 | 1 | 5 | 4 | 3 |
| 1 | 5 | 3 | 2 | 6 | 4 |
| 3 | 1 | 4 | 6 | 2 | 5 |
| 4 | 3 | 2 | 1 | 5 | 6 |
| 5 | 2 | 6 | 4 | 3 | 1 |

(corner clues: 2466, 1456, 2456, 3446, 1345, 1334)

a)

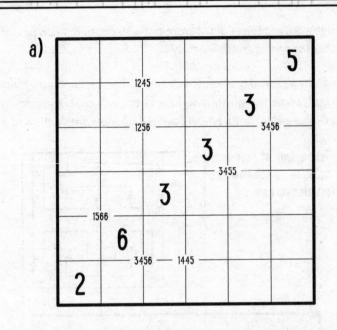

b)

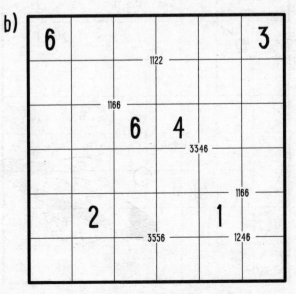

Can you draw a series of separate paths to connect each pair of identical space objects together?

The paths must not cross or touch each other, and no more than one path can enter any grid square. Each path must be made up of only horizontal and vertical lines – diagonals aren't allowed.

Take a look at this example solution to see how the puzzle works:

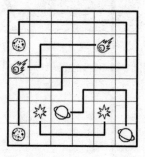

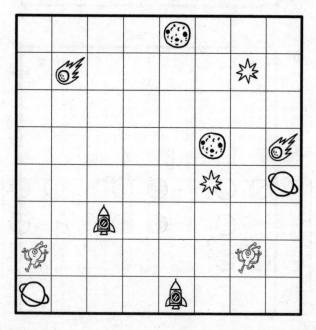

Draw horizontal and vertical lines to join all of the planets into pairs, so that each pair consists of one unshaded and one shaded planet. Lines cannot cross over other planets, nor each other.

Here is an example solution to show you how it works:

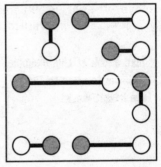

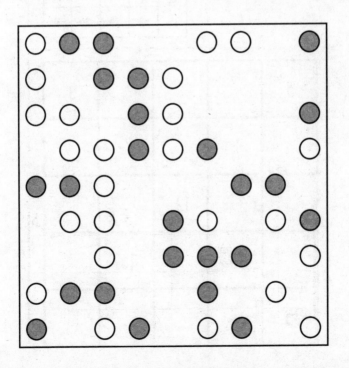

Can you fill in the empty squares so that the grid contains every number from 1 to 25 once each? There is just one rule, which is that you must be able to start at '1' and then move to '2', '3', '4' and so on by moving only to touching grid squares. You can move left, right, up and down between squares, but not diagonally.

Take a look at the example solution to see how it works:

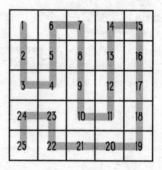

| 3 |  |  |  | 9 |
|---|---|---|---|---|
|  | 1 |  | 7 |  |
|  |  | 19 |  |  |
|  | 23 |  | 13 |  |
| 25 |  |  |  | 15 |

Can you draw along some of the dashed lines to divide this map of a space station into four identical sections, with no unused squares left over?

Each of the four sections must be identical, although they can be rotated versions of each other.

Take a look at the example solution to see how it works:

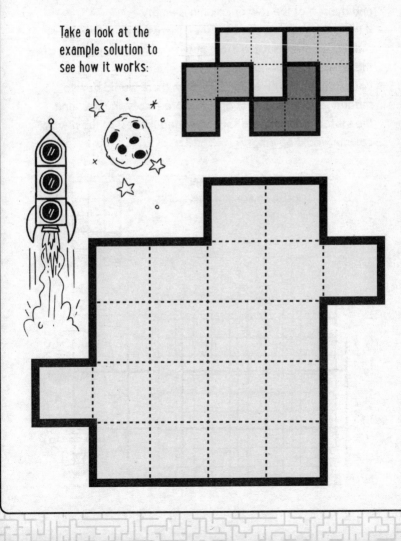

Shade some squares in the image below to reveal a hidden picture. The numbers reveal how many shaded squares there are in each row or column, reading from left to right or top to bottom.

- If there is just one number then this tells you that there are that many touching shaded squares in the row or column, and the rest of the row or column is empty.
- If there are multiple numbers then there are as many sets of shaded squares as there are numbers, with each set being of the length shown - and in the order given.
- For example, if a clue was '2, 3' then there would be two shaded squares, a gap of one or more empty squares, and then three more shaded squares – and the rest of the row or column would be empty.

Take a look at the example solution to see how this works:

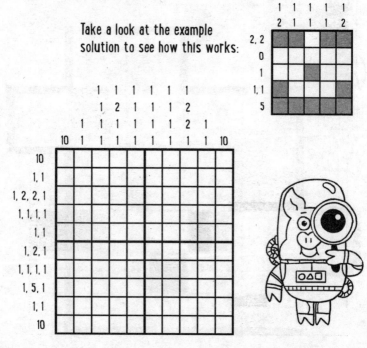

Draw a loop showing the path of a rocket that visits every white square, travelling horizontally or vertically between touching squares. The loop cannot enter any square more than once.

Here is an example to show you how it works:

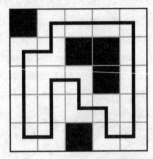

Can you solve this futoshiki puzzle by placing the numbers 1 to 5 once each into every row and column?

You must obey the arrows, which act as 'greater than' signs. The arrows always point from the bigger number to the smaller number of a pair. This means that, for example, you could have '2 > 1' since 2 is greater than 1, but '1 > 2' would be wrong because 1 is not greater in value than 2.

Place a letter from A to F into each empty square in the grid below, so that no letter repeats in any row or column.

Identical letters can't be in touching squares – not even diagonally.

| | | F | E | | |
|---|---|---|---|---|---|
| | | A | B | | |
| D | B | | | A | C |
| F | A | | | E | B |
| | | B | A | | |
| | | C | D | | |

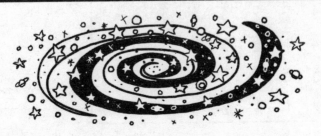

Can you work out how to fit a complete set of dominoes into this grid? The number of spots on the end of each domino is given, but it's up to you to join them into pairs representing the actual domino tiles.

Draw along the dashed lines to show where each domino is placed, and use the chart to keep track of which dominoes you've already used. Each combination of numbers on the two ends of the domino appears exactly once in the grid.

One domino is already drawn in and marked off, to show you how the puzzle works.

| 0 | 1 | 2 | 3 | 4 | 5 | 6 | |
|---|---|---|---|---|---|---|---|
|   |   |   |   |   |   |   | 0 |
|   |   |   | ✓ |   |   |   | 1 |
|   |   |   |   |   |   |   | 2 |
|   |   |   |   |   |   |   | 3 |
|   |   |   |   |   |   |   | 4 |
|   |   |   |   |   |   |   | 5 |
|   |   |   |   |   |   |   | 6 |

| 1 | 2 | 1 | 4 | 6 | 4 | 5 | 0 |
|---|---|---|---|---|---|---|---|
| 6 | 5 | 5 | 0 | 3 | 3 | 5 | 6 |
| 1 | 2 | 0 | 2 | 6 | 1 | 4 | 3 |
| 4 | 0 | 2 | 3 | 3 | 6 | 1 | 4 |
| 4 | 1 | 2 | 6 | 0 | 6 | 5 | 2 |
| 5 | 5 | 2 | 3 | 0 | 0 | 0 | 3 |
| 4 | 1 | 1 | 2 | 4 | 3 | 5 | 6 |

The aim of this puzzle is to place lights into some of the empty grid squares so that every empty white square is lit by at least one light.

- Lights shine along grid squares in the same row or column as far as the first black square they reach. They don't shine diagonally.
- The numbers in the shaded squares tell you exactly how many of the touching squares (above, below, to the left and right) contain lights. A '0' means that no touching squares contain a light.
- A light isn't allowed to shine directly on any other light.
- You can place lights on any empty square so long as the rules are followed – they don't have to be next to the number clues.

Take a look at this example solution. Notice how each white square is lit up by at least one light:

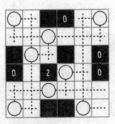

Can you join some of the dots in order to draw the path of a speeding astronaut, travelling from one black dot to the other? The exact number of dots visited in each row and column is given, and the path can only travel horizontally or vertically between dots.

The path cannot cross over any of the shaded squares, and nor can it cross over itself or use a dot more than once.

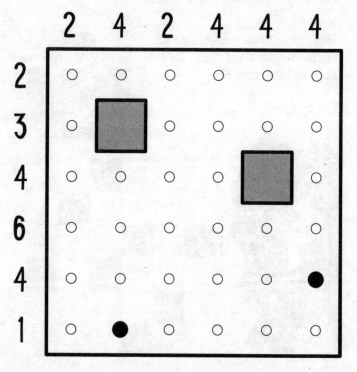

Shade in some squares to make a picture. Each number shows the total number of touching squares — including diagonally touching squares and the square with the number in — that must be shaded.

Take a look at the numbers in this solved example. Notice how they match the number of surrounding shaded squares:

| | | 2 | | 3 |
|---|---|---|---|---|
| 3 | 4 | | | |
| 2 | | 1 | 3 | |
| 3 | | | 5 | |
| | 4 | 3 | | 3 |

| | | 4 | | 4 | | |
|---|---|---|---|---|---|---|
| 5 | 8 | | 7 | | 8 | 5 |
| | 9 | | 8 | | 9 | |
| | | 9 | | 9 | | |
| | 6 | 8 | 9 | 8 | | 3 |
| | | | 7 | | | |
| 0 | 1 | | | | 1 | 0 |

⏱ TIME ..................

Help Robo Mouse place either a '0' or a '1' into each empty square so that there are an equal number of '0's and '1's in each row and column.

You must place the numbers so that there are never more than two '0's or two '1's in succession in any row or column.

Take a look at this example solution to see how it works:

| 1 | 1 | 0 | 0 | 1 | 0 |
|---|---|---|---|---|---|
| 0 | 0 | 1 | 0 | 1 | 1 |
| 0 | 0 | 1 | 1 | 0 | 1 |
| 1 | 1 | 0 | 0 | 1 | 0 |
| 0 | 0 | 1 | 1 | 0 | 1 |
| 1 | 1 | 0 | 1 | 0 | 0 |

| 0 |   |   | 0 |   |   |
|---|---|---|---|---|---|
|   |   |   |   | 1 | 1 |
| 1 | 1 | 0 | 1 |   | 0 |
|   |   | 1 |   |   |   |
| 1 | 1 |   | 1 |   | 0 |
| 1 | 1 | 0 |   |   |   |

Can you help Astro Dog complete this 'no four in a row' game?
Place an 'X' or an 'O' into every empty square, while making
sure that you don't create any lines of four or more 'X's or 'O's in
any direction, including diagonally.

Here's an example
puzzle to show you
how it works:

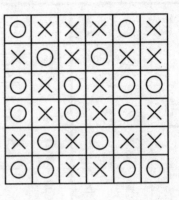

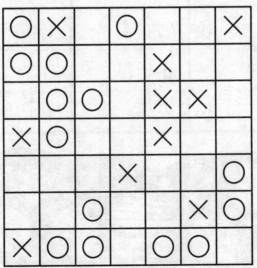

Can you solve this mega sudoku? Place a number from 1 to 9 into every empty square so that no number repeats in any row, column or bold-lined 3×3 box.

| 1 |   | 3 |   |   |   | 2 |   | 6 |
|---|---|---|---|---|---|---|---|---|
|   |   |   | 1 | 6 | 8 |   |   |   |
| 6 |   | 5 |   | 2 |   | 8 |   | 7 |
|   | 3 |   | 2 | 9 | 6 |   | 7 |   |
|   | 6 | 4 | 8 |   | 5 | 3 | 9 |   |
|   | 5 |   | 4 | 1 | 3 |   | 2 |   |
| 3 |   | 8 |   | 4 |   | 1 |   | 5 |
|   |   |   | 6 | 8 | 7 |   |   |   |
| 9 |   | 6 |   |   |   | 7 |   | 2 |

The aim of this puzzle is to draw lines representing rocket flightpaths between the planets.

- Each planet contains a number. Each planet must have the same number of flightpaths connected to it as that number.
- Flightpaths can't cross over other flightpaths or planets.
- There can be no more than two flightpaths between any pair of planets.
- Only horizontal and vertical flightpaths are allowed.

You must arrange the set of flightpaths so that someone could fly from one planet to any other planet, just by using the flightpaths that you've drawn.

Here's an example solution to show you how it works:

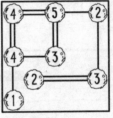

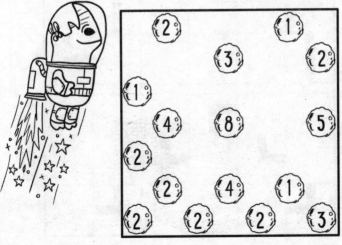

Draw a loop that visits every square of the grid, using only horizontal and vertical lines. In each square, the loop can either pass straight through, turn or cross over itself. Apart from where it crosses over itself, it cannot enter any square more than once. Some squares are already completed, to get you started.

Here's an example solution so you can see how it works:

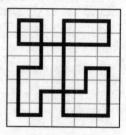

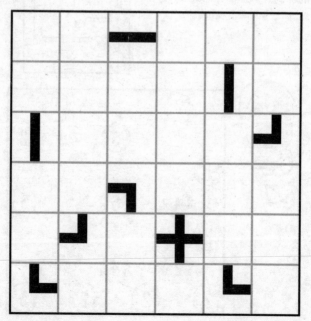

Can you draw a series of separate paths to connect each pair of identical space pictures together?

The paths must not cross or touch each other, and no more than one path can enter any grid square. Each path must be made up of only horizontal and vertical lines — diagonals aren't allowed.

Take a look at the example solution to see how it works:

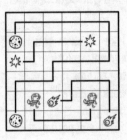

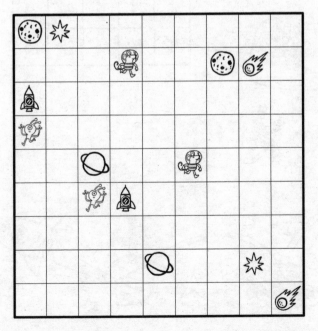

To solve the puzzles on the opposite page, can you plot routes for the spaceship in the empty squares so that each grid contains every number from 1 to 16 once each?

There is just one rule, which is that you must be able to start at '1' and then move to '2', '3', '4' and so on by moving only to touching grid squares, including diagonally touching squares.

Take a look at this example solution to see how it works before trying the two puzzles opposite:

| 10 | 7 | 8 | 2 | 3 |
| 11 | 9 | 6 | 4 | 1 |
| 12 | 13 | 5 | 20 | 21 |
| 16 | 14 | 19 | 22 | 24 |
| 15 | 17 | 18 | 25 | 23 |

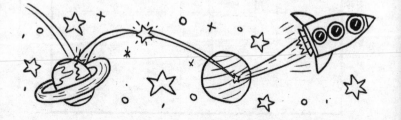

**a)**

|    | 10 |    |    | 15 |
|----|----|----|----|----|
| 8  | 7  | 13 | 14 | 16 |
| 6  |    | 20 | 17 | 22 |
| 3  |    | 18 |    | 23 |
| 4  |    | 1  |    | 25 |

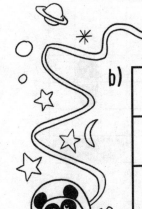

**b)**

| 8  | 10 | 11 | 13 | 14 |
|----|----|----|----|----|
|    | 7  | 12 |    |    |
| 5  |    | 18 | 20 |    |
|    | 25 | 1  | 19 |    |
| 3  | 2  |    | 23 | 22 |

Can you complete the spaceship puzzle on the opposite page by placing the given set of spaceships into the grid? The spaceships are of four different lengths, with one or two spaceships of each length, as shown beneath the puzzle.

- Each row and column has a number next to it. This tells you how many squares in that row or column contain part of a spaceship.
- Spaceships can be placed horizontally or vertically, but not diagonally.
- Spaceships can't be in touching squares, including diagonally touching squares.

This example shows you how it works:

Five spaceship parts have already been placed to get you started.

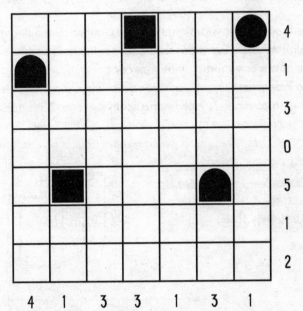

4
1
3
0
5
1
2

4   1   3   3   1   3   1

Place these seven spaceships:

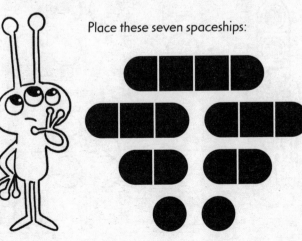

Draw a loop that passes through some of the squares, made up
of horizontal and vertical lines. The loop must visit every square
containing a circle, and cannot enter any square more than once.

- The loop must pass straight through a square containing an
  unshaded circle but then make a turn in the next square either
  as it enters or exits the circle – or both.
- The loop must turn on a square containing a shaded circle,
  but then continue straight in the next square on both sides
  of the circle.

Take a look at this example.
Notice how the unshaded and
shaded circles follow the
rules given above:

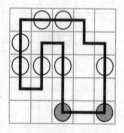

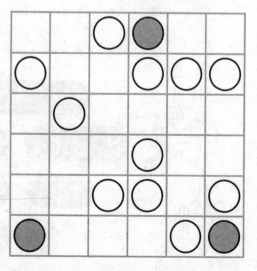

Can you join all of the dots to form a single loop that visits every dot? You can only use straight horizontal or vertical lines to join dots, and the loop can't cross or touch itself. Some parts of the loop have already been drawn in to get you started.

Here's an example solution to show you how it works:

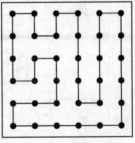

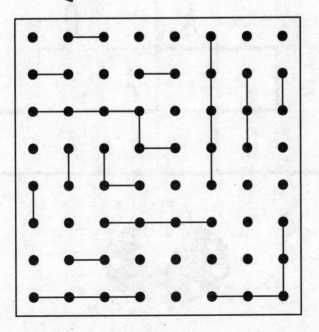

Can you complete this grid so that every row, column and bold-lined region contains each of the letters from A to F once each?

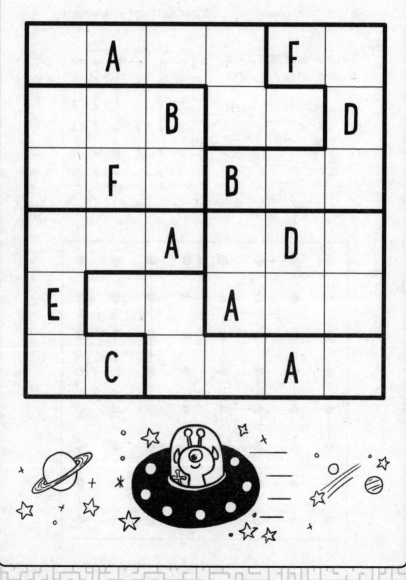

Help the aliens fill in the grid below by placing the letters A, B and C once each into every row and column. This means that there will be two empty squares in each row and column.

The letters outside the grid show which letter appears nearest in their row or column.

Study this example to see how it works:

|   | A | C | B | A | B |   |
|---|---|---|---|---|---|---|
| C |   | C | B | A |   | A |
| A | A |   |   | C | B | B |
| C | C | B | A |   |   | A |
| B | B | A |   |   | C | C |
| C |   |   | C | B | A | A |
|   | B | A | C | B | A |   |

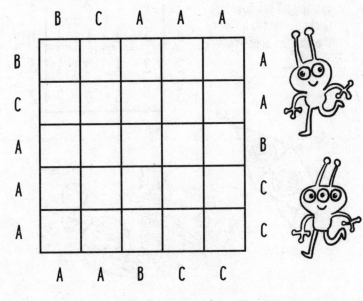

|   | B | C | A | A | A |   |
|---|---|---|---|---|---|---|
| B |   |   |   |   |   | A |
| C |   |   |   |   |   | A |
| A |   |   |   |   |   | B |
| A |   |   |   |   |   | C |
| A |   |   |   |   |   | C |
|   | A | A | B | C | C |   |

Place a digit from 1 to 4 into each square so that no digit repeats in any row or column.

Each digit represents an alien building of that many floors, and the numbers outside the grid reveal the total number of alien buildings that can be 'seen' from the point of view of that number. Taller buildings obscure shorter buildings, but never the other way around.

For example, a clue of '4' must mean that the digits reading away from that number are '1 2 3 4', in that order, so that all four alien buildings can be seen. On the other hand, a clue of '1' means that the digit next to that number must be a '4', since only one alien building can be seen and so it must be the tallest building.

Take a look at the example to see how this works, then try both of the puzzles opposite:

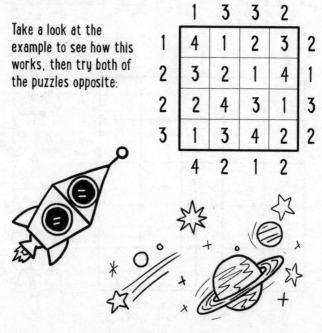

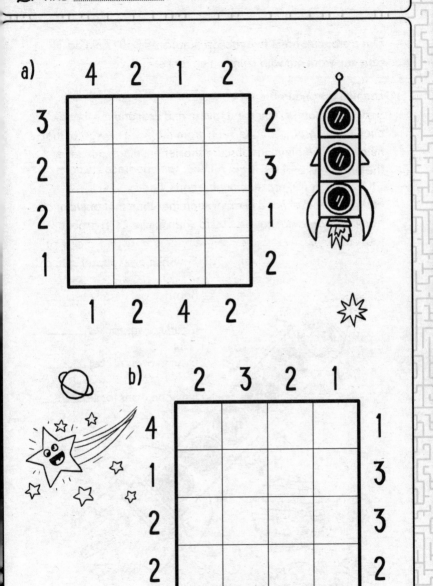

TIME ..................

Five astronauts have five rockets numbered 3, 5, 7, 9 and 11.
Can you work out who owns which rocket?

The five astronauts are:
Anushka, Beatrice, Charlie, Davina and Emiliano.

You also know that:
- Anushka's rocket is a lower number than Beatrice's, who in turn has a lower rocket number than Charlie.
- Charlie's rocket has a number 4 greater than that of Davina.
- Emiliano does not have a rocket with number 3, 5 or 9.

Anushka owns rocket _____

Beatrice owns rocket _____

Charlie owns rocket _____

Davina owns rocket _____

Emiliano owns rocket _____

This puzzle is called 'killer sudoku' because it's a much trickier version of regular sudoku! Not only must you place 1 to 6 once each into every row, column and bold-lined 2x3 box, but you must also solve all of the 'killer clues'.

Each 'killer clue' consists of a number at the top-left of a dashed-line region of grid squares. All the numbers you place in that region must add up to the small number printed in the top left-hand corner of that region. Not only that, but you can't repeat the same number within any dashed-line region.

Shade some squares in the grid opposite to reveal a hidden picture.

- The numbers reveal how many shaded squares there are in each row or column, reading from left to right or top to bottom.
- If there is just one number then this tells you that there are that many touching shaded squares in the row or column, and the rest of the row or column is empty.
- If there are multiple numbers then there are as many sets of shaded squares as there are numbers, with each set being of the length shown – and in the order given.

In this example solution, notice how the clue '1, 2' is made up of one shaded square, a gap and then two more shaded squares:

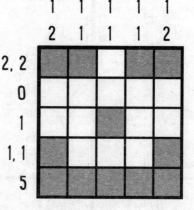

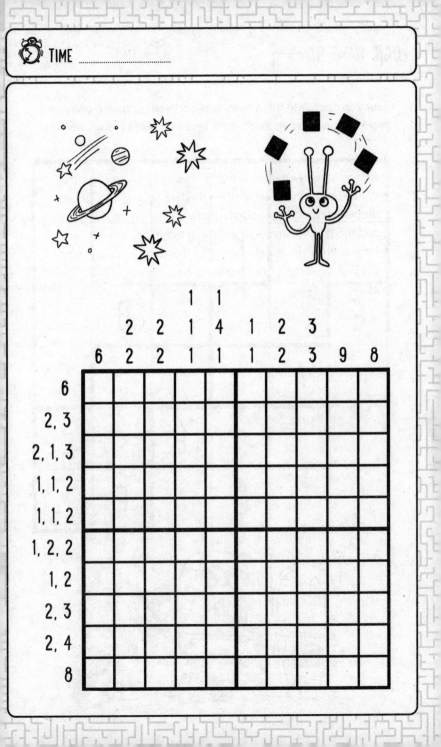

Can you complete this grid so that every row, column and bold-lined region contains all of the letters from A to F once each?

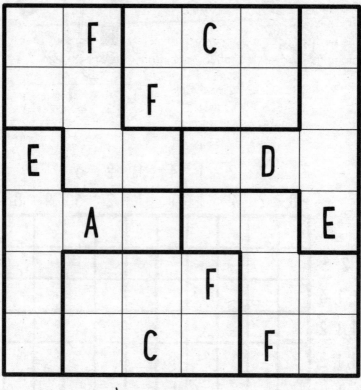

Place a digit from 1 to 6 into each square that does not already contain a number, so no digit repeats in any row, column or 3×2 box.

The puzzle contains three space worms. The digits placed along the body of each space worm must increase by 1 at each step along the body of the space worm, from its tail to its head.

Here's an example solution. Notice how the numbers written along the worms obey this rule: they are '456', '1234' and '234':

| 5 | 2 | 3 | 1 | 6 | 4 |
|---|---|---|---|---|---|
| 6 | 1 | 4 | 2 | 5 | 3 |
| 3 | 5 | 2 | 4 | 1 | 6 |
| 4 | 6 | 1 | 3 | 2 | 5 |
| 1 | 3 | 6 | 5 | 4 | 2 |
| 2 | 4 | 5 | 6 | 3 | 1 |

Hint: Start by working out which numbers go on each worm.

| | | | 1 | 6 | |
|---|---|---|---|---|---|
| | | | | | |
| | | | | | |
| | | | | | |
| | | | | | |
| 1 | | | | | 6 |

Help the animal astronauts solve each of these puzzles, by placing either a shaded or an unshaded circle into every empty square, so that there are no 2x2 (or larger) areas of circles of the same colour.

You must also place the circles so that all those of the same colour connect together. This means that you can travel to any circle of the same colour by moving left, right, up and down between touching squares of the same colour of circle.

Take a look at this example solution, which also shows the connections between touching circles. Notice how there are two areas: one of shaded circles and one of unshaded circles:

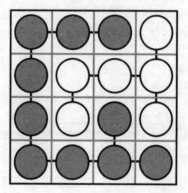

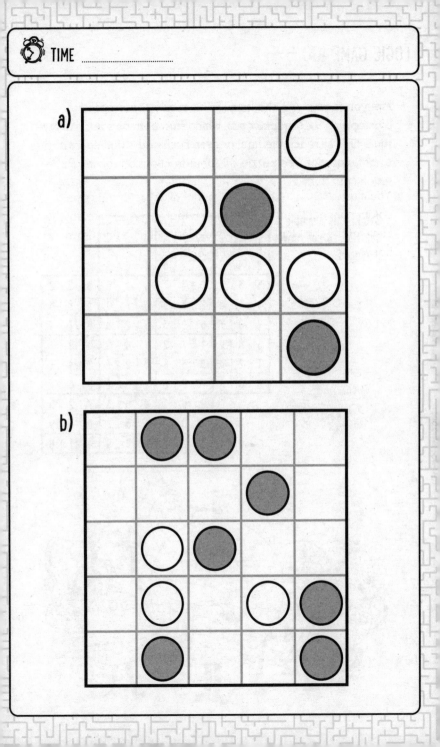

Are you ready for a challenge? This puzzle consists of two overlapping 9x9 sudoku grids, which must both be solved at the same time to reach the final answer. Each grid is outlined with a lighter border. See puzzle 83 for instructions on solving 9x9 sudoku puzzles.

Study this example solution to see how it works:

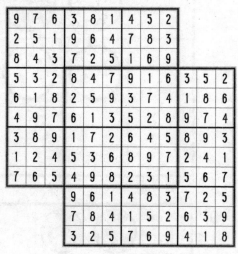

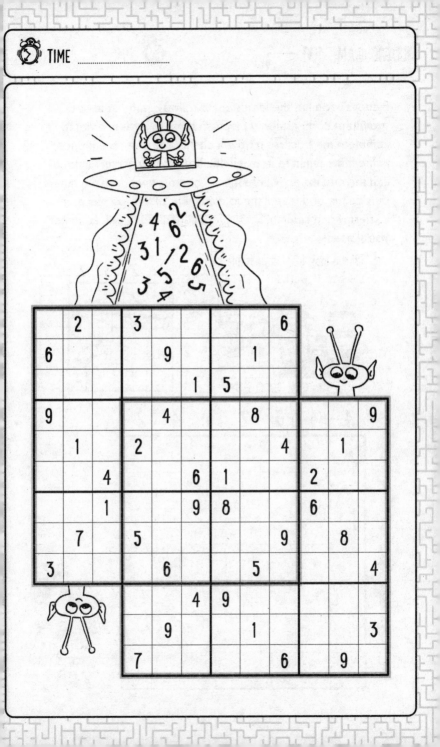

| | 2 | | 3 | | | | | 6 |
| 6 | | | | 9 | | | 1 | |
| | | | | 1 | 5 | | | |
| 9 | | | | 4 | | 8 | | | 9 |
| | 1 | | 2 | | | | 4 | | 1 |
| | | 4 | | 6 | 1 | | 2 | |
| | | 1 | | 9 | 8 | | 6 | |
| | 7 | | 5 | | | | 9 | | 8 |
| 3 | | | 6 | | | 5 | | | 4 |
| | | | 4 | 9 | | | | |
| | | 9 | | | 1 | | | 3 |
| | 7 | | | | | 6 | | 9 |

Planet Zygon has the largest astro-railway in the galaxy. Draw straight or corner railway pieces in some squares in order to complete the track, so it travels all the way from its entrance in the left column to its exit in the bottom row. It can't enter or exit the grid except where shown, or cross over itself. Numbers outside the grid reveal the total number of railway pieces in each row and column. Some pieces are already placed to get you started.

Take a look at this example to see how it works:

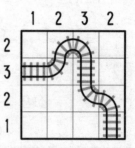

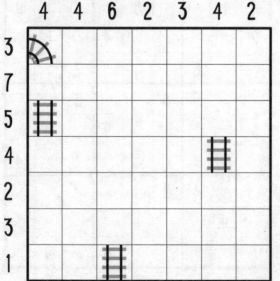

All
of the
ANSWERS

## LOGIC GAME 1

a)

b)

## LOGIC GAME 2

## LOGIC GAME 3

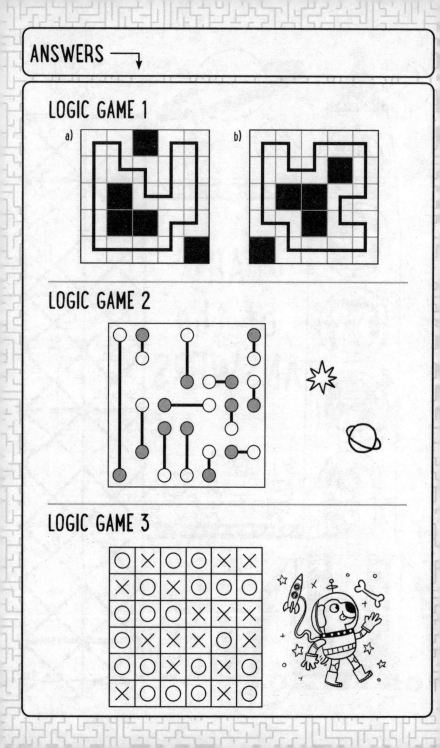

## LOGIC GAME 4

a)

| 3 | 2 | 1 | 4 |
|---|---|---|---|
| 1 | 4 | 3 | 2 |
| 4 | 1 | 2 | 3 |
| 2 | 3 | 4 | 1 |

b)

| 4 | 3 | 1 | 2 |
|---|---|---|---|
| 2 | 1 | 4 | 3 |
| 1 | 2 | 3 | 4 |
| 3 | 4 | 2 | 1 |

## LOGIC GAME 5

a)

| 11 | 12 | 13 | 16 |
|----|----|----|----|
| 10 | 9  | 14 | 15 |
| 7  | 8  | 1  | 2  |
| 6  | 5  | 4  | 3  |

b)

| 4  | 3  | 2  | 1  |
|----|----|----|----|
| 5  | 6  | 7  | 8  |
| 12 | 11 | 10 | 9  |
| 13 | 14 | 15 | 16 |

## LOGIC GAME 6

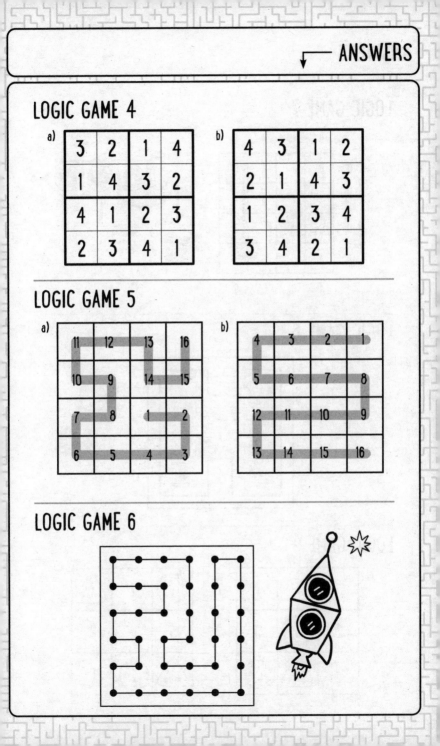

## LOGIC GAME 7

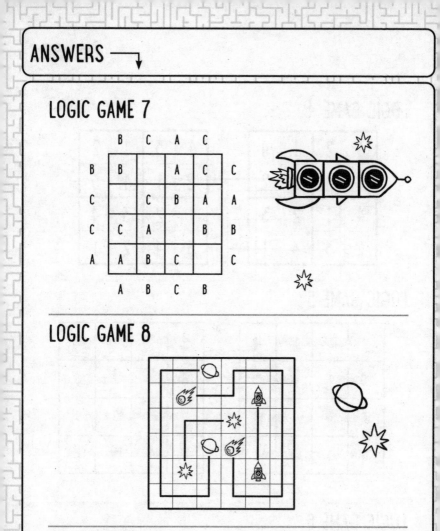

|   | B | C | A | C |   |
|---|---|---|---|---|---|
| B | B |   | A | C | C |
| C |   | C | B | A | A |
| C | C | A |   | B | B |
| A | A | B | C |   | C |
|   | A | B | C | B |   |

## LOGIC GAME 8

## LOGIC GAME 9

a)

|   | 1 | 1 |
|---|---|---|
| 2 | ● | 3 |
|   | △ | ● |

b)

| ● | 2 | △ |
|---|---|---|
| 3 |   | 2 |
| △ | ● | 1 |

## LOGIC GAME 10

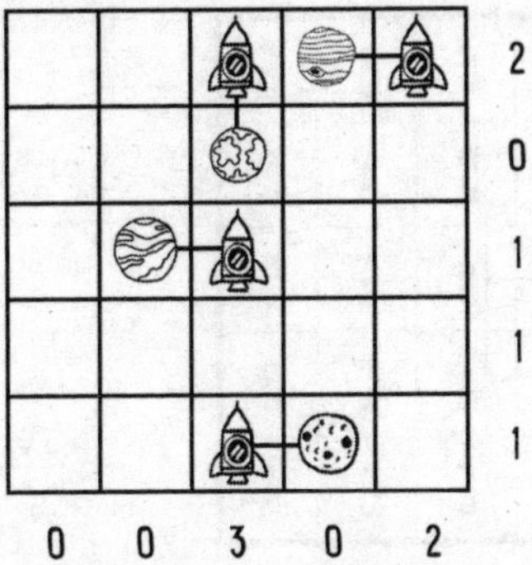

## LOGIC GAME 11

| | | | | |
|---|---|---|---|---|
| D | C | A | E | B |
| B | A | E | C | D |
| E | B | D | A | C |
| A | D | C | B | E |
| C | E | B | D | A |

## LOGIC GAME 12

a)

| | | | |
|---|---|---|---|
| 1 | 4 | 2 | 3 |
| 4 | 2 | 3 | 1 |
| 2 | 3 | 1 | 4 |
| 3 | 1 | 4 | 2 |

2234 — 1233 — 1134

1134

b)

| | | | |
|---|---|---|---|
| 3 | 2 | 1 | 4 |
| 2 | 1 | 4 | 3 |
| 1 | 4 | 3 | 2 |
| 4 | 3 | 2 | 1 |

1124

1124

1344 — 2334

## LOGIC GAME 13

| D | A | C | B | E |
|---|---|---|---|---|
| B | E | D | A | C |
| A | C | B | E | D |
| E | D | A | C | B |
| C | B | E | D | A |

## LOGIC GAME 14

a)

| 2 | 6 | 1 | 3 | 5 | 4 |
|---|---|---|---|---|---|
| 4 | 5 | 3 | 1 | 6 | 2 |
| 3 | 4 | 6 | 2 | 1 | 5 |
| 1 | 2 | 5 | 4 | 3 | 6 |
| 6 | 1 | 2 | 5 | 4 | 3 |
| 5 | 3 | 4 | 6 | 2 | 1 |

b)

| 6 | 4 | 2 | 5 | 1 | 3 |
|---|---|---|---|---|---|
| 5 | 3 | 1 | 2 | 4 | 6 |
| 2 | 5 | 6 | 1 | 3 | 4 |
| 3 | 1 | 4 | 6 | 5 | 2 |
| 1 | 2 | 3 | 4 | 6 | 5 |
| 4 | 6 | 5 | 3 | 2 | 1 |

## LOGIC GAME 15

a)

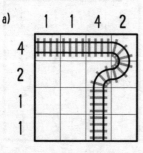

b)

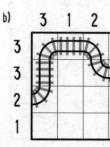

## LOGIC GAME 16

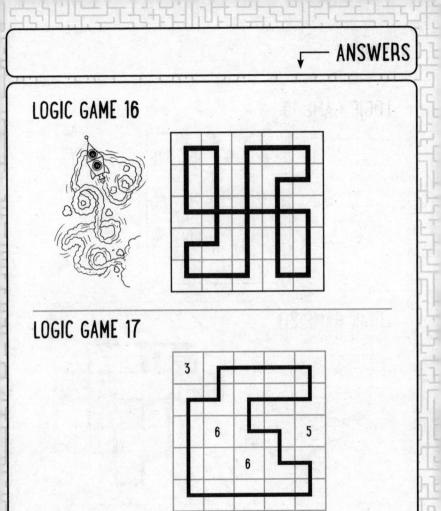

## LOGIC GAME 17

## LOGIC GAME 18

James is 5, Selma is 7 and Marco is 8.

## LOGIC GAME 19

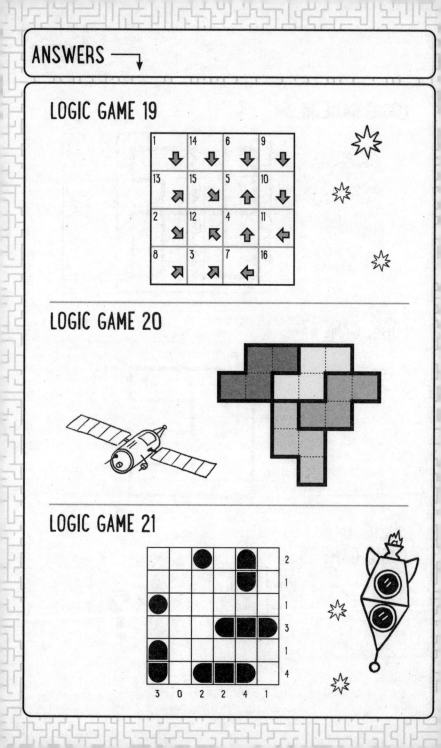

## LOGIC GAME 20

## LOGIC GAME 21

## LOGIC GAME 22

a)

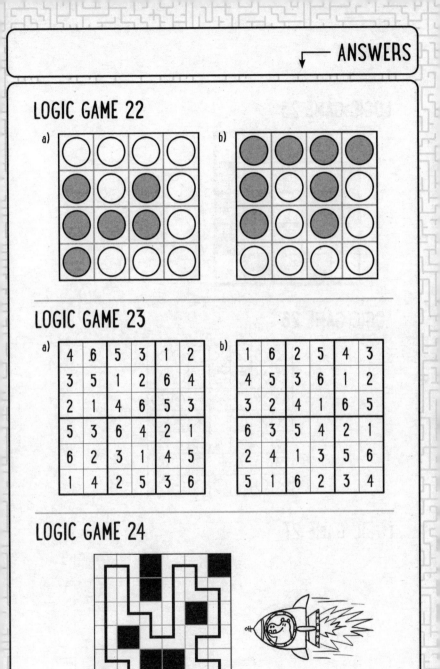

## LOGIC GAME 23

a)

| 4 | 6 | 5 | 3 | 1 | 2 |
|---|---|---|---|---|---|
| 3 | 5 | 1 | 2 | 6 | 4 |
| 2 | 1 | 4 | 6 | 5 | 3 |
| 5 | 3 | 6 | 4 | 2 | 1 |
| 6 | 2 | 3 | 1 | 4 | 5 |
| 1 | 4 | 2 | 5 | 3 | 6 |

b)

| 1 | 6 | 2 | 5 | 4 | 3 |
|---|---|---|---|---|---|
| 4 | 5 | 3 | 6 | 1 | 2 |
| 3 | 2 | 4 | 1 | 6 | 5 |
| 6 | 3 | 5 | 4 | 2 | 1 |
| 2 | 4 | 1 | 3 | 5 | 6 |
| 5 | 1 | 6 | 2 | 3 | 4 |

## LOGIC GAME 24

## LOGIC GAME 25

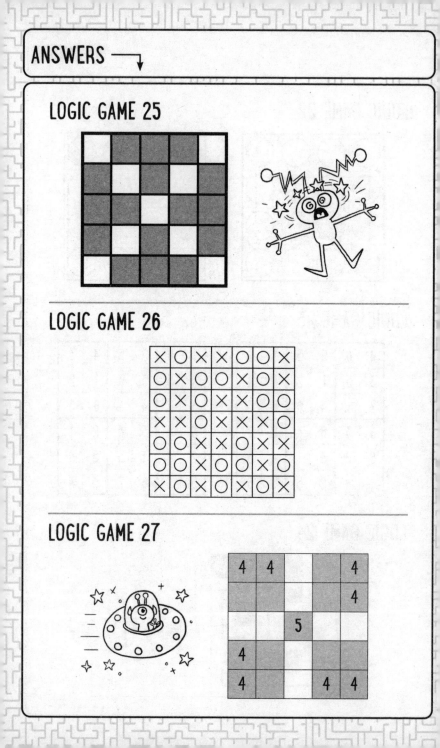

## LOGIC GAME 26

| × | ○ | × | × | ○ | ○ | × |
|---|---|---|---|---|---|---|
| ○ | × | ○ | ○ | × | ○ | × |
| ○ | × | ○ | × | × | ○ | ○ |
| × | × | ○ | × | × | × | ○ |
| ○ | ○ | × | × | ○ | × | × |
| ○ | ○ | × | ○ | ○ | × | ○ |
| × | ○ | × | ○ | × | ○ | × |

## LOGIC GAME 27

| 4 | 4 |   |   | 4 |
|---|---|---|---|---|
|   |   |   |   | 4 |
|   |   | 5 |   |   |
| 4 |   |   |   |   |
| 4 |   |   | 4 | 4 |

# LOGIC GAME 28

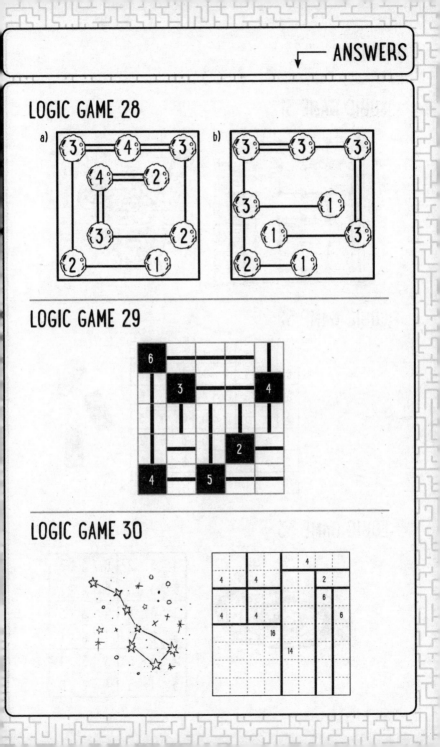

# LOGIC GAME 29

# LOGIC GAME 30

## LOGIC GAME 31

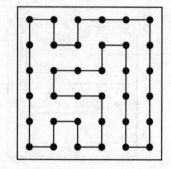

## LOGIC GAME 32

| 6 | 2 | 4 | 5 | 1 | 5 | 5 | 1 |
|---|---|---|---|---|---|---|---|
| 6 | 5 | 5 | 2 | 1 | 1 | 0 | 4 |
| 5 | 0 | 0 | 3 | 4 | 3 | 4 | 6 |
| 3 | 4 | 6 | 2 | 0 | 0 | 5 | 3 |
| 4 | 4 | 2 | 2 | 0 | 6 | 6 | 2 |
| 1 | 3 | 3 | 3 | 5 | 6 | 4 | 6 |
| 0 | 3 | 1 | 1 | 0 | 2 | 2 | 1 |

## LOGIC GAME 33

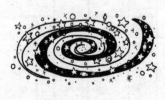

| 4 | 5 | 2 | 6 | 1 | 3 |
|---|---|---|---|---|---|
| 6 | 3 | 1 | 5 | 4 | 2 |
| 1 | 6 | 4 | 2 | 3 | 5 |
| 5 | 2 | 3 | 1 | 6 | 4 |
| 2 | 4 | 6 | 3 | 5 | 1 |
| 3 | 1 | 5 | 4 | 2 | 6 |

# LOGIC GAME 34

a)

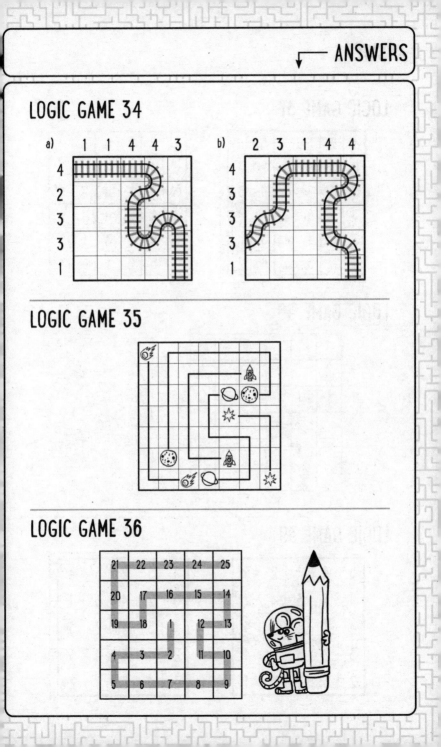

b)

# LOGIC GAME 35

# LOGIC GAME 36

| 21 | 22 | 23 | 24 | 25 |
|----|----|----|----|----|
| 20 | 17 | 16 | 15 | 14 |
| 19 | 18 | 1  | 12 | 13 |
| 4  | 3  | 2  | 11 | 10 |
| 5  | 6  | 7  | 8  | 9  |

## LOGIC GAME 37

a)

| 4 | 2 | 3 | 1 | 5 | 6 |
|---|---|---|---|---|---|
| 6 | 3 | 4 | 5 | 2 | 1 |
| 5 | 1 | 2 | 6 | 4 | 3 |
| 3 | 5 | 6 | 2 | 1 | 4 |
| 2 | 6 | 1 | 4 | 3 | 5 |
| 1 | 4 | 5 | 3 | 6 | 2 |

b)

| 1 | 2 | 6 | 5 | 3 | 4 |
|---|---|---|---|---|---|
| 6 | 4 | 3 | 2 | 5 | 1 |
| 5 | 3 | 1 | 4 | 2 | 6 |
| 3 | 1 | 5 | 6 | 4 | 2 |
| 2 | 6 | 4 | 3 | 1 | 5 |
| 4 | 5 | 2 | 1 | 6 | 3 |

## LOGIC GAME 38

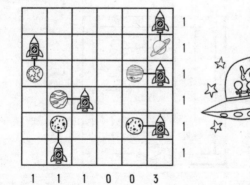

## LOGIC GAME 39

a)

| 5 | 4 | 1 | 2 | 3 |
|---|---|---|---|---|
| 1 | 5 | 3 | 4 | 2 |
| 4 | 1 | 2 | 3 | 5 |
| 3 | 2 | 5 | 1 | 4 |
| 2 | 3 | 4 | 5 | 1 |

b)

| 1 | 3 | 2 | 5 | 4 |
|---|---|---|---|---|
| 5 | 2 | 4 | 3 | 1 |
| 4 | 5 | 1 | 2 | 3 |
| 2 | 1 | 3 | 4 | 5 |
| 3 | 4 | 5 | 1 | 2 |

## LOGIC GAME 40

| 0 | 1 | 0 | 0 | 1 | 1 |
|---|---|---|---|---|---|
| 0 | 0 | 1 | 0 | 1 | 1 |
| 1 | 0 | 1 | 1 | 0 | 0 |
| 0 | 1 | 0 | 0 | 1 | 1 |
| 1 | 0 | 1 | 1 | 0 | 0 |
| 1 | 1 | 0 | 1 | 0 | 0 |

## LOGIC GAME 41

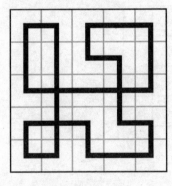

## LOGIC GAME 42

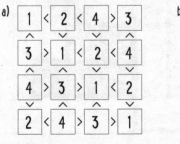

a)

| 1 | < | 2 | < | 4 | > | 3 |
|---|---|---|---|---|---|---|
| ∧ | | ∨ | | ∨ | | ∧ |
| 3 | > | 1 | < | 2 | < | 4 |
| ∧ | | ∧ | | ∨ | | ∨ |
| 4 | > | 3 | > | 1 | < | 2 |
| ∨ | | ∧ | | ∧ | | ∨ |
| 2 | < | 4 | > | 3 | > | 1 |

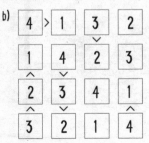

b)

| 4 | > | 1 | | 3 | | 2 |
|---|---|---|---|---|---|---|
| | | | | ∨ | | |
| 1 | | 4 | | 2 | | 3 |
| ∧ | | ∨ | | | | |
| 2 | | 3 | | 4 | | 1 |
| ∧ | | ∨ | | | | ∧ |
| 3 | | 2 | | 1 | | 4 |

## LOGIC GAME 43

- Luis is drawing an astronaut using a felt pen.

- Isabella is drawing a rocket using a ballpoint pen.

- Shivani is drawing a moonscape using a fountain pen.

## LOGIC GAME 44

| 2 | 🍪 | 3 | 🔺 | 1 |
|---|---|---|---|---|
| 3 | 🔺 | 3 | 2 | |
| 🔺 | 3 | 2 | 1 | 🍪 |
| 2 | 🍪 | 1 | | 2 |
| 1 | | 1 | | 🍪 |

## LOGIC GAME 45

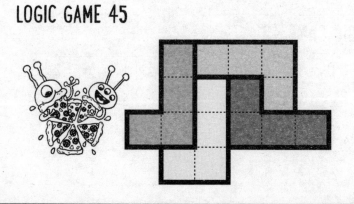

## LOGIC GAME 46

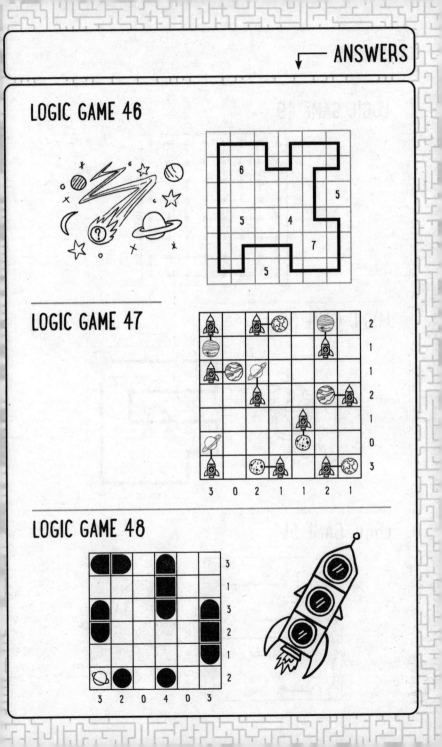

## LOGIC GAME 47

## LOGIC GAME 48

## LOGIC GAME 49

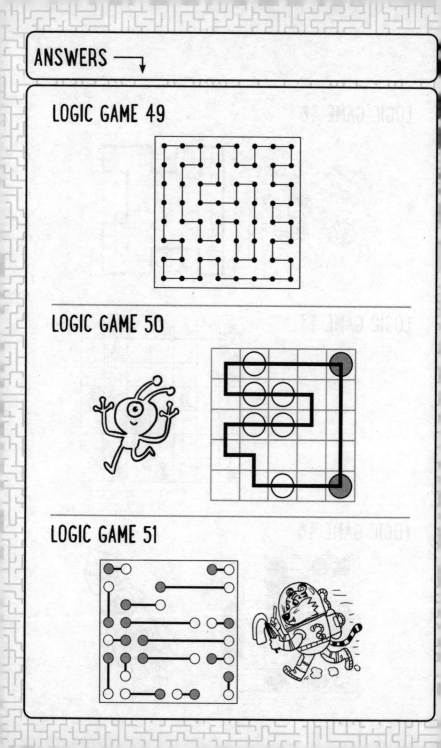

## LOGIC GAME 50

## LOGIC GAME 51

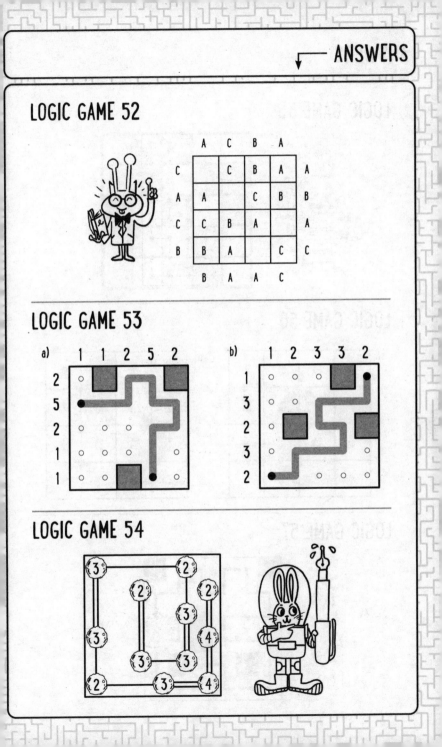

# LOGIC GAME 52

|   | A | C | B | A |   |
|---|---|---|---|---|---|
| C |   | C | B | A | A |
| A | A |   | C | B | B |
| C | C | B | A |   | A |
| B | B | A |   | C | C |
|   | B | A | A | C |   |

# LOGIC GAME 53

a)

|   | 1 | 1 | 2 | 5 | 2 |
|---|---|---|---|---|---|
| 2 |   |   |   |   |   |
| 5 |   |   |   |   |   |
| 2 |   |   |   |   |   |
| 1 |   |   |   |   |   |
| 1 |   |   |   |   |   |

b)

|   | 1 | 2 | 3 | 3 | 2 |
|---|---|---|---|---|---|
| 1 |   |   |   |   |   |
| 3 |   |   |   |   |   |
| 2 |   |   |   |   |   |
| 3 |   |   |   |   |   |
| 2 |   |   |   |   |   |

# LOGIC GAME 54

## LOGIC GAME 55

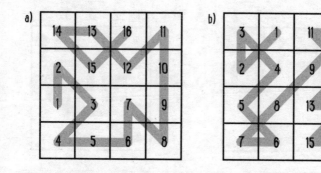

## LOGIC GAME 56

a)

| 14 | 13 | 16 | 11 |
|----|----|----|----|
| 2  | 15 | 12 | 10 |
| 1  | 3  | 7  | 9  |
| 4  | 5  | 6  | 8  |

b)

| 3 | 1 | 11 | 10 |
|---|---|----|----|
| 2 | 4 | 9  | 12 |
| 5 | 8 | 13 | 14 |
| 7 | 6 | 15 | 16 |

## LOGIC GAME 57

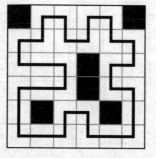

# ANSWERS

## LOGIC GAME 58

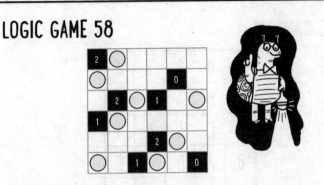

## LOGIC GAME 59

| 1 | 2 | 6 | 4 | 5 | 3 |   |   |
|---|---|---|---|---|---|---|---|
| 6 | 4 | 5 | 3 | 1 | 2 |   |   |
| 3 | 5 | 2 | 1 | 6 | 4 |   |   |
| 4 | 3 | 1 | 6 | 2 | 5 | 3 | 4 |
| 2 | 6 | 3 | 5 | 4 | 1 | 6 | 2 |
| 5 | 1 | 4 | 2 | 3 | 6 | 5 | 1 |

| 5 | 1 | 6 | 2 | 4 | 3 | 5 | 1 |
|---|---|---|---|---|---|---|---|
| 2 | 3 | 5 | 4 | 1 | 6 | 3 | 2 |
| 6 | 4 | 1 | 3 | 2 | 5 | 6 | 4 |
|   |   | 3 | 1 | 5 | 4 | 2 | 6 |
|   |   | 2 | 6 | 3 | 1 | 4 | 5 |
|   |   | 4 | 5 | 6 | 2 | 1 | 3 |

## LOGIC GAME 60

| 1 | 3 | 4 | 0 | 3 | 3 | 6 | 1 |
|---|---|---|---|---|---|---|---|
| 1 | 5 | 6 | 2 | 1 | 1 | 6 | 4 |
| 0 | 4 | 3 | 2 | 5 | 5 | 1 | 5 |
| 6 | 2 | 3 | 3 | 1 | 6 | 2 | 2 |
| 6 | 0 | 6 | 0 | 2 | 0 | 5 | 3 |
| 1 | 4 | 5 | 3 | 0 | 4 | 4 | 2 |
| 5 | 6 | 4 | 2 | 0 | 0 | 4 | 5 |

## LOGIC GAME 61

| A | D | C | E | B |
|---|---|---|---|---|
| E | B | A | D | C |
| D | C | E | B | A |
| B | A | D | C | E |
| C | E | B | A | D |

## LOGIC GAME 62

## LOGIC GAME 63

a)

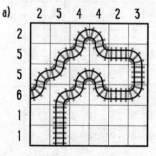

b)

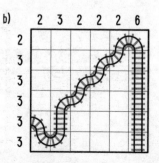

## LOGIC GAME 64

a)
```
      3  1  2
   2  1  3  2  2
   2  2  1  3  1
   1  3  2  1  3
      1  2  2
```

b)
```
      1  3  2
   1  3  1  2  2
   3  1  2  3  1
   2  2  3  1  2
      2  1  2
```

## LOGIC GAME 65

a)
```
2  4  1  3
1  3  4  2
4  2  3  1
3  1  2  4
```

b)
```
2  3  4  1
4  1  3  2
3  2  1  4
1  4  2  3
```

## LOGIC GAME 66

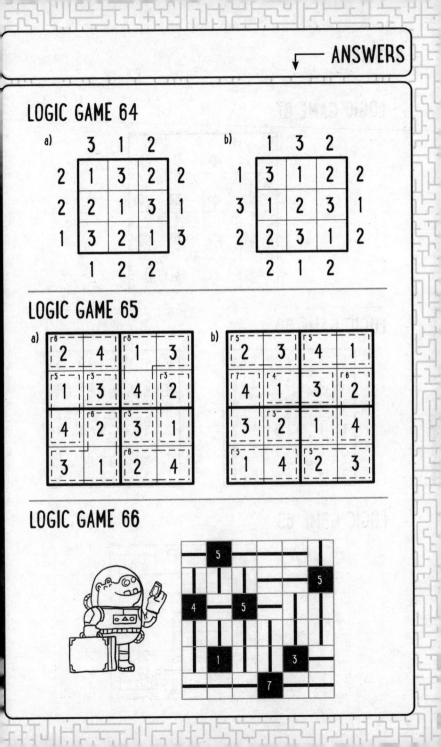

## LOGIC GAME 67

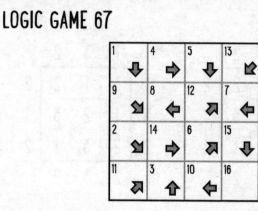

## LOGIC GAME 68

a)

| 3 | 4 | 2 | 6 | 1 | 5 |
|---|---|---|---|---|---|
| 4 | 5 | 1 | 2 | 3 | 6 |
| 1 | 2 | 6 | 3 | 5 | 4 |
| 6 | 1 | 3 | 5 | 4 | 2 |
| 5 | 6 | 4 | 1 | 2 | 3 |
| 2 | 3 | 5 | 4 | 6 | 1 |

b)

| 6 | 4 | 2 | 1 | 5 | 3 |
|---|---|---|---|---|---|
| 3 | 6 | 1 | 2 | 4 | 5 |
| 5 | 1 | 6 | 4 | 3 | 2 |
| 2 | 5 | 4 | 3 | 6 | 1 |
| 4 | 2 | 3 | 5 | 1 | 6 |
| 1 | 3 | 5 | 6 | 2 | 4 |

## LOGIC GAME 69

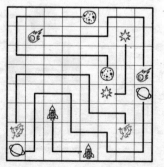

## LOGIC GAME 70

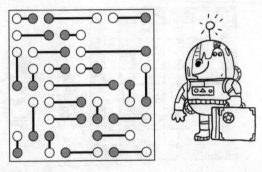

## LOGIC GAME 71

| | | | | |
|---|---|---|---|---|
| 3 | 4 | 5 | 8 | 9 |
| 2 | 1 | 6 | 7 | 10 |
| 21 | 20 | 19 | 12 | 11 |
| 22 | 23 | 18 | 13 | 14 |
| 25 | 24 | 17 | 16 | 15 |

## LOGIC GAME 72

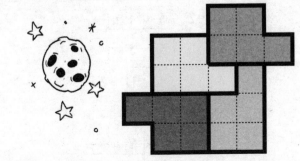

## LOGIC GAME 73

A face

## LOGIC GAME 74

## LOGIC GAME 75

| 5 | 2 | 3 < | 4 > | 1 |
|---|---|---|---|---|
| 2 > | 1 | 5 | 3 | 4 |
| 3 | 5 > | 4 | 1 | 2 |
| 4 | 3 | 1 < | 2 | 5 |
| 1 | 4 | 2 < | 5 > | 3 |

## LOGIC GAME 76

| B | D | F | E | C | A |
|---|---|---|---|---|---|
| E | C | A | B | D | F |
| D | B | E | F | A | C |
| F | A | D | C | E | B |
| C | E | B | A | F | D |
| A | F | C | D | B | E |

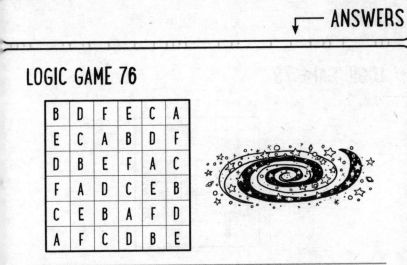

## LOGIC GAME 77

| 1 | 2 | 1 | 4 | 6 | 4 | 5 | 0 |
|---|---|---|---|---|---|---|---|
| 6 | 5 | 5 | 0 | 3 | 3 | 5 | 6 |
| 1 | 2 | 0 | 2 | 6 | 1 | 4 | 3 |
| 4 | 0 | 2 | 3 | 3 | 6 | 1 | 4 |
| 4 | 1 | 2 | 6 | 0 | 6 | 5 | 2 |
| 5 | 5 | 2 | 3 | 0 | 0 | 0 | 3 |
| 4 | 1 | 1 | 2 | 4 | 3 | 5 | 6 |

## LOGIC GAME 78

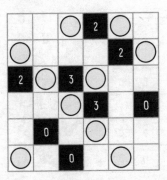

## LOGIC GAME 79

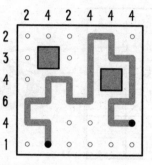

## LOGIC GAME 80

A heart

| | | 4 | | 4 | | |
|---|---|---|---|---|---|---|
| 5 | 8 | | 7 | | 8 | 5 |
| | 9 | | 8 | | 9 | |
| | | 9 | | 9 | | |
| | 6 | 8 | 9 | 8 | | 3 |
| | | | 7 | | | |
| 0 | 1 | | | | 1 | 0 |

## LOGIC GAME 81

| 0 | 0 | 1 | 0 | 1 | 1 |
|---|---|---|---|---|---|
| 0 | 0 | 1 | 0 | 1 | 1 |
| 1 | 1 | 0 | 1 | 0 | 0 |
| 0 | 0 | 1 | 0 | 1 | 1 |
| 1 | 1 | 0 | 1 | 0 | 0 |
| 1 | 1 | 0 | 1 | 0 | 0 |

# LOGIC GAME 82

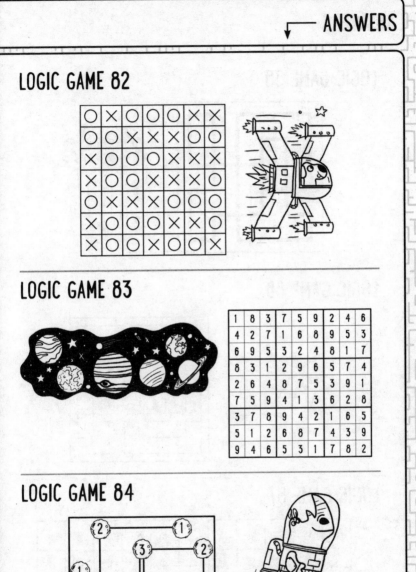

# LOGIC GAME 83

# LOGIC GAME 84

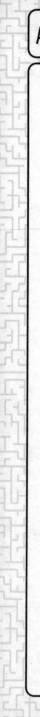

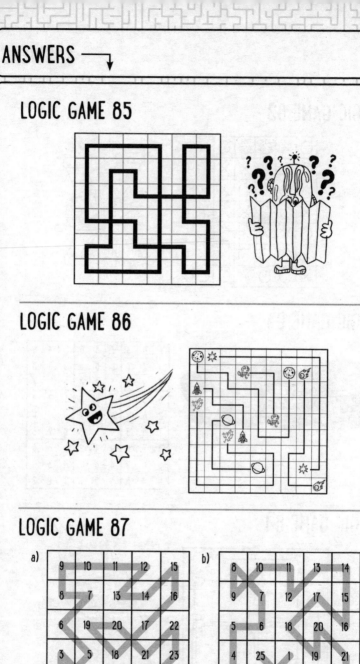

# LOGIC GAME 85

# LOGIC GAME 86

# LOGIC GAME 87

a)

| 9 | 10 | 11 | 12 | 15 |
|---|----|----|----|----|
| 8 | 7 | 13 | 14 | 16 |
| 6 | 19 | 20 | 17 | 22 |
| 3 | 5 | 18 | 21 | 23 |
| 4 | 2 | 1 | 24 | 25 |

b)

| 8 | 10 | 11 | 13 | 14 |
|---|----|----|----|----|
| 9 | 7 | 12 | 17 | 15 |
| 5 | 6 | 18 | 20 | 16 |
| 4 | 25 | 1 | 19 | 21 |
| 3 | 2 | 24 | 23 | 22 |

## LOGIC GAME 88

## LOGIC GAME 89

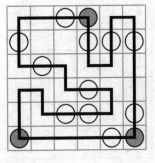

## LOGIC GAME 90

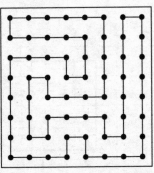

## LOGIC GAME 91

| B | A | E | D | F | C |
|---|---|---|---|---|---|
| A | E | B | F | C | D |
| C | F | D | B | E | A |
| F | B | A | C | D | E |
| E | D | C | A | B | F |
| D | C | F | E | A | B |

## LOGIC GAME 92

|   | B | C | A | A | A |   |
|---|---|---|---|---|---|---|
| B | B | C |   | A |   | A |
| C | C |   |   | B | A | A |
| A |   |   | A | C | B | B |
| A | A | B | C |   |   | C |
| A |   | A | B |   | C | C |
|   | A | A | B | C | C |   |

## LOGIC GAME 93

a)

|   | 4 | 2 | 1 | 2 |   |
|---|---|---|---|---|---|
| 3 | 1 | 3 | 4 | 2 | 2 |
| 2 | 2 | 4 | 3 | 1 | 3 |
| 2 | 3 | 1 | 2 | 4 | 1 |
| 1 | 4 | 2 | 1 | 3 | 2 |
|   | 1 | 2 | 4 | 2 |   |

b)

|   | 2 | 3 | 2 | 1 |   |
|---|---|---|---|---|---|
| 4 | 1 | 2 | 3 | 4 | 1 |
| 1 | 4 | 3 | 1 | 2 | 3 |
| 2 | 3 | 4 | 2 | 1 | 3 |
| 2 | 2 | 1 | 4 | 3 | 2 |
|   | 3 | 2 | 1 | 2 |   |

## LOGIC GAME 94

- Anushka owns rocket 3.

- Beatrice owns rocket 7.

- Charlie owns rocket 9.

- Davina owns rocket 5.

- Emiliano owns rocket 11.

## LOGIC GAME 95

| 4 | 1 | 5 | 2 | 3 | 6 |
| 6 | 3 | 4 | 1 | 5 | 2 |
| 5 | 2 | 3 | 6 | 1 | 4 |
| 2 | 6 | 1 | 5 | 4 | 3 |
| 3 | 5 | 2 | 4 | 6 | 1 |
| 1 | 4 | 6 | 3 | 2 | 5 |

## LOGIC GAME 96

A clock

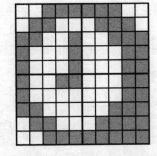

## LOGIC GAME 97

| D | F | E | C | A | B |
|---|---|---|---|---|---|
| A | E | F | D | B | C |
| E | C | B | A | D | F |
| F | A | D | B | C | E |
| C | B | A | F | E | D |
| B | D | C | E | F | A |

## LOGIC GAME 98

| 2 | 4 | 1 | 6 | 3 | 5 |
|---|---|---|---|---|---|
| 5 | 3 | 6 | 1 | 2 | 4 |
| 6 | 2 | 4 | 5 | 1 | 3 |
| 3 | 1 | 5 | 4 | 6 | 2 |
| 4 | 6 | 2 | 3 | 5 | 1 |
| 1 | 5 | 3 | 2 | 4 | 6 |

## LOGIC GAME 99

a)
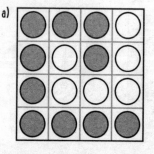

b)
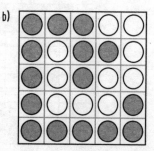

## LOGIC GAME 100

| 1 | 2 | 7 | 3 | 5 | 8 | 9 | 4 | 6 | | | |
|---|---|---|---|---|---|---|---|---|---|---|---|
| 6 | 8 | 5 | 7 | 9 | 4 | 3 | 1 | 2 | | | |
| 4 | 9 | 3 | 6 | 2 | 1 | 5 | 7 | 8 | | | |
| 9 | 3 | 6 | 1 | 4 | 7 | 2 | 8 | 5 | 3 | 6 | 9 |
| 7 | 1 | 8 | 2 | 3 | 5 | 6 | 9 | 4 | 8 | 1 | 7 |
| 2 | 5 | 4 | 9 | 8 | 6 | 1 | 3 | 7 | 2 | 4 | 5 |
| 5 | 6 | 1 | 4 | 7 | 9 | 8 | 2 | 3 | 6 | 5 | 1 |
| 8 | 7 | 2 | 5 | 1 | 3 | 4 | 6 | 9 | 7 | 8 | 2 |
| 3 | 4 | 9 | 8 | 6 | 2 | 7 | 5 | 1 | 9 | 3 | 4 |
| | | | 3 | 5 | 4 | 9 | 7 | 8 | 1 | 2 | 6 |
| | | | 6 | 9 | 8 | 5 | 1 | 2 | 4 | 7 | 3 |
| | | | 7 | 2 | 1 | 3 | 4 | 6 | 5 | 9 | 8 |

## LOGIC GAME 101

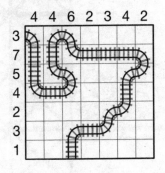

NOTES
AND
SCRIBBLES

# ALSO AVAILABLE:

ISBN 9781780556192

ISBN 9781780556185

ISBN 9781780555638

ISBN 9781780555935

ISBN 9781780555621

ISBN 9781780556635

ISBN 9781780554730

ISBN 9781780554723

ISBN 9781780555409

ISBN 9781780556208

ISBN 9781780553146

ISBN 9781780553078

ISBN 9781780553085

ISBN 9781780552491